147 Practical Tips for Using Experiential Learning

Co-written and co-edited by

William M. Timpson, Jeffrey M. Foley,
Nathalie Kees, and Alina M. Waite

Atwood Publishing
Madison, WI

147 Practical Tips for Using Experiential Learning
Edited by William M. Timpson, Jeffrey M. Foley, Nathalie Kees, and Alina M. Waite

ISBN: 978-1-891859-92-2

Cover design by Tamara Dever, TLC Graphics: www.tlcgraphics.com

Timpson, William M.
  147 tips for using experiential learning / co-written and co-edited by William M. Timpson, Jeffrey M. Foley and Nathalie Kees and Alina M. Waite.
       pages cm.
  Includes bibliographical references and index.
  ISBN 978-1-891859-92-2 (pb)
  1. Active learning. 2. Experiential learning. I. Title. II. Title: One hundred forty-seven tips for using experiential learning.
  LB1027.23.T56 2013
  371.3—dc23
                                    2013047005

ACKNOWLEDGMENTS

We want to thank the following individuals for contributing to this volume.

Christine Aguilar

Catherine Black

Lynne Celli

Gailmarie Kimmel

Jacqueline McGinty

Eden Haywood-Bird

Margit Hentschel

Leann Kaiser

Deanna Leone

Melanie Nichols

Nereida Perdigon

Lisa Pitot

Melanie Ramey

Nicholas Young

Goldlin Wall

Lowell Wightman

We also want to thank our publisher, Linda Babler, at Atwood Publishing for her support and guidance, as well as Kathryn A. Wright for her contributions as copy editor.

FOREWORD

Experiential education is often wrongly considered as a single method, rather than a philosophy that informs many methods (Itin 1999). In this book Timpson, Foley, Kees, and Waite correctly position *147 Practical Tips for Using Experiential Learning* in the context of an informing set of ideas linked to a range of methods. The book is both practical and thought provoking. The reader is invited to explore the underlying theoretical elements of the philosophy of experiential education and to utilize specific activities in enhancing experiential learning opportunities for students. The concise nature of each of the "tips" lends itself to choosing one or two tips on which to focus, rather than being compelled to digest the entirety of the book.

This book has value to both the new teacher and to the seasoned professional. Even those who currently are well versed in experiential education will find value in the thought provoking refresher on the nature of how to increase or deepen experiential education. For those looking for a book of activities, this is not that book; rather it is a book that will allow any teacher to more effectively use the growing number of "activity" books on the market (which often include little or no informing philosophy).

In this manner, *147 Practical Tips for Using Experiential Learning* fills a much needed gap in the literature about what informs the use of activity in educational practice. The book makes clear that activity, in and of itself, is not experiential education (it may not even be experiential learning). Rather, for there to be experiential education, a huge range of philosophical tenets must be considered. While there are activities discussed, they are contextualized in a broader philosophical purpose and intent.

I am grateful to the authors for taking the time to gather and develop a set of tips that will help teachers in any setting from primary to secondary and higher education, and even to educators in nontraditional settings such as youth programs, ministry programs, and more. I welcome the addition of this resource in the growing evolution of the work on experiential education.

Dr. Christian M. Itin, is Chair and Professor of the Department of Social Work at Metropolitan State University of Denver. Among many other professional and personal accomplishments, Dr. Itin served as the President of the Board of Directors for the Association for Experiential Education.

TABLE OF CONTENTS

INTRODUCTION: OUR EXPERIENCES

As we begin this volume of tips for using experiential learning, we want to share our sources of inspiration, all those who push theory into practice, who insist on more holistic and hands-on learning, who want to challenge individuals of all ages to better trust their interactions with the world and learn how to arrive at their own conclusions, to innovate and even rethink what they have been told or taught. While we cite those like David Kolb who have long been writing about experiential learning, we also draw on many others—Piaget and Bruner who have described the developmental emergence of physical, visual, and linguistic capabilities and argued for more hands-on learning; researchers like Howard Gardner who advocate for more holistic, multisensory learning; all those scholars who want more student-centered, inductive learning where awareness and constructivist thinking are emphasized over memorized knowledge; and all those who want us to challenge people to better align their actions with their values.

As we developed this manuscript on experiential learning, we thought it important for you, the reader, to know something about our backgrounds as teachers, practitioners, and scholars, what drew us together to research and write the ideas and the "tips" we offer here. Our own experiences and training represent very different disciplines—educational psychology (Bill Timpson), adult education and training (Jeff Foley), counseling (Nathalie Kees), and human resource development (Alina Waite). We deliberately threw the net wide to invite in the synergy that sparks innovation. Yet, despite coming from different backgrounds and disciplines, we also have much in common. Each of us has extensive classroom experiences with traditional approaches to instruction and we know our strengths and weaknesses. Most important, however, is that each of us also has an eagerness to learn, to explore and experience new terrain as instructors in order to better engage students in whatever will deepen their learning, whatever will prove more engaging and meaningful.

In addition, we will share our own stories of discovery, how experiences have shaped our thinking, and what this means for our teaching.

Experiences: Bill Timpson

Born and raised in Roxbury, Massachusetts, a predominantly African American community just south of downtown Boston, I experienced my early years as a "majority-minority" in a city that would later explode in racial violence over busing. I "experienced" diversity directly without having any special skills other than what the progressive values of my parents offered. My mom had been a union organizer in the textile industry during the Great Depression, once famously arrested in Georgia for daring to speak before a mixed audience of whites and blacks. My dad was a tunnel worker on crews that reflected the multi-ethnic nature of the city, no matter how segregated the various communities were from each other, or how deep their racist roots and teachings.

When the civil rights movement put the fight for racial equality into our living room with the televised evening news of the segregated south and the protests, police, arrests, dogs, and fire hoses, my parents were among the earliest supporters of desegregation. They saw the need for solidarity within the working classes and talked about the early history of the labor movement and the place for mass action. More directly for me, an all-American kind of baseball-playing boy, I was out in the street celebrating with all my friends when the Brooklyn Dodgers and Jackie Robinson won the World Series in 1955 and blasted a huge hole in the all-white history of "America's pastime." Our Little League team was, of course, the Dodgers.

Sports represented one of those experiences where kids could cross ethnic, class, and religious divides and quickly bond as teammates, no matter their differences or the prejudices that were learned at home. Whatever was taught in those ethnic enclaves—how "our" people were better than "others"—could be just as quickly unlearned in the grind of football or basketball practices when we aligned with whoever lined up next to us, first against the coaches and then against other teams.

Inside the classrooms, of course, many unspoken lessons in the hidden curriculum went far beyond the academic content. Along with reading, mathematics, social studies, science, and foreign languages, we also learned to sit quietly—or else. We learned to get our homework done on time and correctly—or else. I learned that one B+ amongst A's in the fourth grade would arouse my father's anger. Overall, my experiences in school were positive because I fit in and did well, although some of my friends struggled, and these experiences undermined their self-confidence, at least about the place for education in their future.

In college, across town at Harvard, my experiences in class were more of the same, although lectures were large and we only handed in papers or assignments infrequently. Again, with classmates from across the country and some from overseas, we bonded through sports and our residential experiences, eating meals together, going to dances on the weekends, heading out for an 11 pm roast beef sandwich at Elsie's, learning to play bridge in the afternoons, working part time at a Boy's Club nearby. These experiences beyond the classroom intensified as the protests against the Vietnam War heated up and the talk over meals invariably turned to ways to avoid the draft. As the world erupted into protest and young people seemed to be in the forefront of the press for change, my classes seemed dull and too often divorced from the reality outside.

Getting a teaching job in the inner city of Cleveland meant a sea change of experiences, from sitting and studying to standing and correcting, from organizing my own schedule to taking on responsibility for 150-plus rambunctious adolescents in the largest junior high school in Ohio. When I arrived to teach, the east side of Cleveland was still smoldering from the riots of the summer of 1968, following the assassination of Martin Luther King, Jr., when police and local citizens were killed in shootouts and entire blocks were set on fire, the Black Panthers were active, and the Junior Black Panthers paraded around our school. Teaching was, above all else, a daily emotional trial by fire.

Moving on to graduate school at the University of Wisconsin-Madison after four years was another sea change of experiences. I had to sell off almost everything I had acquired to return to full-time student status. While my undergraduate major in history was more of a general background, my studies in educational psychology were directly related to my just-completed teaching experiences—how students could best learn, especially within the cultural divides of ethnicity and social class.

Accepting a tenure track position at Colorado State University meant another shift in experience—new town, new responsibilities, new colleagues and friends, new projects, and more. Directing a large federally-funded Teacher Corps Project from 1978-1981 meant more changes and new experiences we visited other projects in other states—the Pine Ridge Reservation schools and the challenges facing the Lakota people in South Dakota, the needs of Hispanic kids in Utah whose parents had immigrated, some legally and some not, to do the toughest and poorest paid work. At our national meetings, we listened to reports of efforts to improve schools for low income students across the country.

Receiving a National Kellogg Fellowship Award meant extensive experiences overseas from 1981-1984. During the six weeks I spent in Nicaragua I studied their literacy campaign, which also gave me the opportunity to simultaneously experience life as a second language learner living with a family in Managua. How frustrating it was to be limited in communication to such a primitive level because my own Spanish language skills were so meager! I was also able to visit Cuba on a study tour and experience first hand a hospitality, warmth, and heart felt nationalism that was in striking contrast to the official line in the Reagan White House, which condemned everything about that island nation and seemed very threatened by Fidel Castro's regime and its commitment to alternative socio-political and economic principles. Additional experiences in China, Europe, and Brazil remain memorable today, some thirty-plus years later.

The experience of directing Centers for Teaching and Learning at three different research universities from 1991-2003 meant new experiences, obstacles, and challenges. What worked best for me was to join with colleagues in different disciplines in order to explore the challenges that they were facing and what might help. Invariably, I would share ideas about experiential learning that could energize their classes and deepen student learning.

Reconnecting with a childhood friend who was the CEO of restaurant chains—at first it was Au Bon Pain and then Uno Chicago Grill—I found common ground in the value of teaching and learning for energizing a business—encouraging the exploration that underlies innovation, the coaching that can make real a commitment to ongoing improvement, and the formative feedback that is essential for a "learning organization" to become real. In those early years, we had to invest much time in my re-education through extended visits to different restaurant sites to interview key staff there, experiences that helped me integrate my expertise from the world of education into the business world.

In a similar way, my two Fulbright Senior Specialist awards for peace and reconciliation studies have allowed me to experience other cultures in ways that go far beyond what could be captured only through reading. In Northern Ireland in 2006, I was able to spend six weeks and visit the sites of so much violence over so many years, interview people on both sides of the divide, and collaborate with scholars interested in supporting a sustainable peace process. In Burundi, Africa, I was able to visit the University of Ngozi in 2011, teaching a variety of courses on restorative justice, sustainability, peace, and reconciliation, while consulting with those who had survived forty years of genocide, civil war, and violence and now wanted to build a better future for themselves and their country.

Looking back over a long and productive career in education, I can see the advantages of experiential learning for my own understanding as well as in what I can use to deepen the understanding of my students. In my fifteen books on various aspects of teaching, learning, and professional development, as well as in various chapters and articles, there has always been a consistent thread emphasizing experiential learning. For example, I continue to take my classes through our campus ropes/challenge course and give students a first-hand opportunity to experience and process challenges that usually arouse real fear and anxiety, despite the safety equipment that they wear. I continue to require service learning projects where students have to take what they learn into the field, work with others, and evaluate the results. I continue to emphasize discovery learning, in which complete immersion in a case study can fully engage all the senses and deepen learning. I continue to use field trips and activities to add variety to the classroom and energize students. I also learn a lot about my students and their learning styles and preferences when I observe them in different environments.

At the core of my teaching (and learning) practice there is a dynamic and essential interrelationship between direct instruction and experiential learning. At times, concepts and skills will be taught, but then hands-on experiences and applications are needed to drive learning deeper. At other times, I might lead with an activity and then use direct instruction to explain the underlying concepts. In the context of Bloom's hierarchy, direct instruction can efficiently be used to cover lots of information—the lowest "knowledge" level—and in very large classes. However, moving into higher levels—understanding, application, analysis, synthesis and evaluation—typically requires more activity on the part of the student, trying out ideas and learning from mistakes—i.e., experiential learning.

WILLIAM M. TIMPSON, PhD
Professor, School of Education 105E, Colorado State University, Fort Collins, CO 80523. PHONE: 970.4891.7630. FAX: 970.491.1317.
William.Timpson@colostate.edu

Experiences: Jeffrey M. Foley

As a high school graduation gift from my parents I completed a 23 day mountaineering course with the Colorado Outward Bound School in the summer of 1986. This experience had a profound impact on my life and altered the course of my professional path. I was a third generation sprinkler fitter (those little fire sprinklers in the ceiling of your office) from Detroit. My grandfather put the first fire sprinklers in Henry Ford's plant. My father was a fitter, and so was my uncle. I had started to work in the shop in preparation to go to apprenticeship school. Don't get me wrong—working as a pipe fitter is an honorable trade and I really enjoyed being part of a tradition. But the mountaineering experience with nine other kids and two amazing instructors in the heart of Rocky Mountain country had a tremendous impact on my self-world view—that collection of experiences, biases, and assumptions that ultimately serve as the frame through which I interpret and interact with the world.

My self-world view up until I graduated high school in 1986 was strongly informed by my family, my schooling, my church, and my community—as is the case for many of us. I was born in the heat of the Detroit riots in 1968. Throughout my childhood we were participants in "white flight," a phenomenon where middle class white families would incrementally move farther and farther away from inner-city Detroit as their financial situation improved. The community in which we ended up was very conservative, very white, and very racist. Not having many other perspectives shared with me during my teens, I did not know of many realities outside of my upbringing and small community.

When I started my Outward Bound experience I had quite a few reservations about being put into an ethnically and racially diverse group of teens. It was not that I had a hatred or anger toward other people I perceived as different from myself—I was just scared. I had never been exposed to different cultures or ethnicities, and I feared the unknown. One of the tips I offer in this book is about drawing a tension between the known and the unknown so that learning can happen. My Outward Bound instructors were able to recognize my discomfort and instead of judging me for my self-world view, they created opportunities for me to interact in a safe and healthy manner, to challenge the basic assumptions that had been guiding me for the entirety of my young adult life, to learn from those experiences, and to make changes in my self-world view, thus creating changes in how I interacted authentically with others. Through this process I changed—physically, mentally, and emotionally —and I was able to move forward in life with these new skills and attitudes. This opened up many new possibilities for how I could interact with the world. The process that these instructors used to guide my transformation was experiential education. And from that day on I would study, research, and incorporate this teaching and learning method into every aspect of my life.

I jumped ship from the sprinkler-fitter trade and dove head first into outdoor adventure and experiential education. I wanted to work as an Outward Bound instructor, and I explored every avenue possible to accomplish that goal. I had many excellent mentors along the way. Rodney Ley, the director of the Outdoor Adventure Program at CSU, took me under his wing and provided many opportunities to work as a rock climbing guide, ice climbing guide, and ski instructor in the backcountry of Colorado. At the same time, I joined the local search and rescue unit and launched into a parallel career that would last twenty years, along with my mountain-guiding career. After four years of working for small guiding outfits, I was finally an instructor for Outward Bound.

My first course was run out of Marble, Colorado—the birth place of Outward Bound in the United States in 1961. Although it was June, there was six feet of snow on the ground for this course. Nine eager teenagers stepped off the bus eyes wide, short of breath, and anxious about what lay ahead. This group of kids was remarkably similar in make-up to those in the course I had taken years before. On one of the first nights as an OB instructor, all of my training and ideas about facilitating learning through experiential techniques were put to the test. We had chosen cooking teams to prepare each meal so that the students could get to know others in the patrol. On this first night the team was made up of Leon and Alice. Leon was a young African American student who had spent the majority of his first thirteen years of life living on the streets of New Orleans. His meals often came from the streets; he had never cooked a meal. He would later tell me that his trip to Colorado for this course was his first time out of inner-city New Orleans. On the bus ride to the airport he saw a cow for the first time. Each and every experience he was having on this trip was very new and very exciting.

Alice came from Melbourne, Australia, and from considerable wealth. This was evident in the top-of-the-line outdoor clothing that she wore, in her mannerisms, and in how she interacted with others. Alice would later share with me that her family had employees who made her bed each day, cooked, cleaned, and facilitated her daily routine. She had never cooked a meal. The simple meal that I was helping them prepare for the group was much more than a pot of macaroni and cheese; it was the first experience for both of these kids in relating to a person from a radically different self-world view. We had a wonderful experience making that dinner, learning about each other, and breaking down many perceived barriers to interacting in this new community. Neither of these kids had ever cooked their own meal before, but the circumstances around that reality were very different. That difference is the magic that makes each of us unique; experiential learning is the avenue that helps us explore those differences and find new meaning.

I went on to instruct hundreds of Outward Bound courses, and serve as a course director, a program manager, and finally as the director of the Rocky Mountain region. My colleagues were some of the most passionate, gifted, and creative facilitators of learning that I have had the pleasure of working with. I also served as an instructor in outdoor leadership at the local community college during this time. I was fortunate enough to take a three year break from Outward Bound to serve as the coordinator of the Outdoor Studies Program at Colorado Mountain College. In the same time frame, I worked my way through the ranks of emergency services in several communities. I worked as an emergency medical technician, a rock and ice rescue technician, a wildland fire fighter, a HAZMAT operator, as a sworn law enforcement officer, and even a member of a SWAT team.

My career in emergency services opened my eyes to an entirely different aspect of experiential education. Emergency services workers face an interesting aspect to their work—they are often asked to step into potentially dangerous work environments where the threat of injury or death is very real. I have trained hundreds of entry-level emergency services workers in many different job tasks. How to make the training *real* and directly applicable to my students' work environment was a continual challenge for me. There was a place for traditional learning in their training (memorization of drug interactions, the indoctrination of policy and procedure), but the majority of the learning was experiential. What was interesting about this type of training was the need to take into account many different cognitive levels at one time. Each student had to master the basic physical tasks (starting an IV, rigging a pulley system) and at the same time develop situation awareness (rockfall, violent patients, gunfire) and stay conscious of his or her emotional state (fear, excitement, confusion) as the event unfolded. For me this was the ultimate in experiential education as the multiplicity of the learning outcomes and the methods to explore those outcomes were very complex. These elements, taken together, challenge the facilitator to develop the ability to track multiple dimensions of learning at one time.

My career as an experiential educator and as an emergency services technician came to an end in 2009. During the seven years leading up to this transition, I earned at CSU a master's degree in education and human resources studies (2004) specializing in adult education and training, and a doctorate in education and human resource studies (2009) with a specialization in community college leadership. I often refer to my graduate experience as the total deconstruction of Jeff Foley. I say that because I had to challenge many of the basic assumptions that I held around teaching, learning, assessment, evaluation, instructional design, and other aspects of instruction. By taking the risk of deconstructing my beliefs, schemas, and mental frame surrounding the teaching and learning experience, I was able to allow many new and exciting concepts and resources to fill my instructional toolbox. I now serve as an assistant professor in Instructional Leadership at the School of Education at Colorado State University, and I love every minute of it!

End result: my experiences as an outdoor educator, emergency services technician, and university professor allowed me to continually challenge my self-world view. Specifically I am able to strive continually to improve my facilitation skills. I believe Sir Edmund Hillary expressed it best in his memoirs about being the first to climb Mount Everest (with Tenzing Norgay): "I have had the good fortune to meet Queens and Princes, Presidents and Prime Ministers, but more importantly for me I have made close friendships with many people from a variety of cultures."

Contributing to this book has been a great exercise in critical reflection, collaboration, philosophical elasticity, and friendship. I hope that some of these tips can help you in your day-to-day instruction.

JEFFREY M. FOLEY, PhD
Assistant Professor, School of Education, Colorado State University, Fort Collins, CO 80523. Phone: 970.491.6289. Fax: 970.491.1317.
Jeffrey.Foley@colostate.edu

Experiences: Nathalie Kees

Growing up on a dairy farm in rural Wisconsin, I had a fairly isolated and insular upbringing. The primary source of difference and animosity in our region seemed to be between the German Catholics (Us) and the German Lutherans (Them). As the middle child of a large hard-working family, I developed a good deal of empathy and caring for animals, others who were less fortunate, and the underdog. As a first generation college student, I "escaped" to St. Norbert College for my undergraduate education, a mere 20 minutes away from home, yet the beginning of a long and continuing journey of self-exploration and learning about others.

As a music teacher in Wisconsin, Maryland, and Wyoming, I learned the intricacies of experiential learning and helping young people learn to sing and play instruments. As a school counselor in Wyoming and a licensed professional counselor in Colorado, I used experiential techniques to help clients see new ways of dealing with difficult situations. And as a counselor educator at Colorado State University for the past twenty-five years, I have continued my journey as a teacher of a skills-based, experiential curriculum, focused on teaching individual and group counseling skills for counselors and teachers in training. Training as a challenge/ ropes course facilitator at Colorado State University provided me with additional resources and techniques for working with experiential groups.

One of my vivid memories from my ropes course training was my realization that I was willing to trust others more so than myself. The realization came to me as I was falling backward from a height of six feet into the arms of my co-trainees without a worry or care that they might not catch me. On the other hand, while climbing a forty-foot pole to put up equipment and having to fasten myself to the pole with carabineers as I went, I began to realize how difficult it was for me to trust that I had done it correctly and was truly safe. This fear and uncertainty left as I gained more experience and self-trust, and I have never forgotten that lesson in trusting myself, as well as others. I did notice that I then had to work on my trust of the equipment as the final part of that process.

My writing and research has been focused in the areas of group facilitation and group counseling, particularly the area of women's groups. I have served as a consultant on group facilitation to groups at Colorado State University, as well as local and state school districts and other agencies such as hospice. After taking a summer workshop with me on group facilitation skills for teachers, one teacher with twenty years of experience said, "I've been teaching all of these years and never realized before that I was working with a group." It is this type of realization that keeps me going, teaching group facilitation skills that can help turn a classroom of individuals into an enriched group experience for the learners as well as the teacher. It is those skills and techniques I hope to share in this book.

Teaching primarily skills-based courses, I use experiential learning all of the time. Students in my classes are required to experience and demonstrate both individual and group counseling skills, to provide themselves and each other with feedback, and to record their practice and demonstrate their expertise. I also created a course called Contemplative Practices in Counseling and Education, which I have offered in a three week summer format. We meet for three hours each day and a good deal of our time is spent experiencing contemplative practices from the major spiritual traditions, including mindfulness based practices from Buddhism, Yoga Nidra meditation from Hinduism, Sufi dream analysis, and Centering Prayer from Christianity. We also have used a local labyrinth to experience walking meditation in the ancient practice of pilgrimage from Catholicism. Students are asked to reflect on their experiences both individually and in group discussions. The practices are facilitated by mental health professionals with backgrounds in their specific spiritual tradition or practice. These presenters also share the historical and philosophical foundation for the spiritual tradition and the contemplative practice.

One of my primary goals in this current book of experiential tips is to help teachers and group facilitators gain an understanding of the skills needed to facilitate effectively the reflective portion of experiential activities. Oftentimes teachers have excellent skills for conducting activities, but lack the skills necessary to process the learning. Skills to draw out group members without "calling on" them include having the group sit in a circle so they can all see each other, using open-ended questions and appropriate wait time, and scanning the group and making eye contact with those who might indicate they are ready to share.

Helping group facilitators break old habits (such as answering their own questions, looking only at the group member who is speaking and not scanning the rest of the group for reactions, and putting group members on the spot by calling on them) has been a particularly rewarding part of my work with counselors and teachers over the years.

NATHALIE KEES, EdD, LPC
Associate Professor, School of Education 224, Colorado State University, Fort Collins, CO 80523. Phone: 970.4891.6720. Fax: 970.491.1317. Nathalie.Kees@ColoState.EDU

Experiences: Alina M. Waite

Reflecting on my past, I recognize that two trips, among other things, were pivotal in guiding my studies, helping develop my personal and professional goals, and ultimately influencing who I have become. I first traveled outside the United States when I was eight years old. Visiting relatives on my father's side of the family and touring many famous sites in England sparked my desire to travel more extensively. A couple of years after this trip, but before entering high school, I traveled to Albuquerque, NM to visit my grandma and see where my mother grew up. I received a T-shirt with the University of New Mexico logo as a souvenir. At that time I never would have guessed UNM would become my Alma-Mater.

I declared Electrical Engineering with a Biomedical Engineering option as my major after my first year of college at UNM, not fully understanding what opportunities might lie ahead for me at that time, but appreciating the fact it combined my passions for math, science, and medicine. I worked as a Graduate Research Assistant in the microbiology and anatomy departments, where I was given the opportunity to conduct research first-hand. Interestingly, my fondest memories of college are of times spent outside the classroom, physically engaged in and leading activities, while working in the laboratories, playing sports, and socializing with family and friends. It was from these occasions I learned to make the most sense of the world, people, and my surroundings.

After graduating from college, I faced a difficult choice between continuing on to graduate school and traveling Europe. I had already accumulated and saved sufficient frequent flyer miles to obtain a free round-trip ticket to fly first-class anywhere in Europe, which was my dream for many years. I wanted to visit other countries and experience their cultures, taste their foods, and meet their people. After receiving sound advice from my mother, I applied and was accepted to the Biomedical Engineering Department at the New Jersey Institute of Technology. To this day I hold that the decision to earn a master's degree first was one of the best I ever made.

My time at graduate school was mostly spent in the orthopedics department at the University of Medicine and Dentistry of New Jersey working on my thesis. Once again, with the aid of my advisors, input from fellow students, and support from family, I navigated the highs and lows of conducting research first-hand. I learned from my mistakes and celebrated my successes, while all in all I strived to expand the knowledge base of my discipline. My sense of reward from my experiences of working in the laboratory was much more rich and enduring than any immediate relief I felt after passing an exam taken inside a classroom. As true today as it was back then, I learn best when I am actively engaged, either working independently or in groups, rather than sitting idle as a bystander regardless of my location.

I eventually realized my long awaited trip to backpack in Europe. Shortly thereafter, I returned to Italy to fulfill my dream of living and working abroad, which also marked the beginning of my career in research and development of medical devices. I stayed in Italy for five years before continuing employment at an American subsidiary of the same company. My experiences as an expatriate were at times challenging, but always enriching, providing learning opportunities for both me and my colleagues. I still recall my first day of work, turning on my computer to find prompts in Italian, and glancing at scholarly journals with articles written in French, Italian, English, and Russian. I found this somewhat overwhelming, albeit amusing, since I only ever studied Spanish in high school. I recall taking time each day after work to study Italian, but my efforts to learn vocabulary, sentence structure, and the like seemed fruitless when confronted with the need to speak. I finally came to the realization that studying in combination with making mistakes while communicating with others would prove most effective in helping me learn a second language.

In addition, our industry made vital use of experiential learning in several ways. Company sponsored training workshops were held for orthopedic surgeons from around the world, serving as venues for them to share their experiences, ideas, and understandings. Lectures were typically followed by hands-on workshops, where surgeons practiced what they learned in a simulated environment. Similar training sessions were held for sales representatives to learn the fundamentals of new product offerings. Conferences and trade shows provided opportunities for information sharing among surgeons, engineers, and management. Such exchanges often led to improvements of existing products and new product ideas. I also realize a key to creative thinking and innovation was collaboration with others from outside our discipline. Inter-disciplinary teams were tasked to identify synergies that would lead to the next "big" ideas needed to propel our organization forward.

Engineers commonly attended surgeries to act as participant observers while surgeons used our products on patients. It was sometimes only possible in the real-world setting of the operating room to understand design limitations, gain alternative perspectives for ways to improve surgical procedures, and envision opportunities in which new and innovative products and services could extend beyond traditional practices in order to make a difference in people's lives. Many factors were of course considered in the decision-making process of whether or not we pursued a new idea; business realities and environmental pressures often weighed heavily in the mix.

I spent over fifteen years working in healthcare prior to returning to school to earn a doctoral degree in organization development. I spent much of this time serving in a variety of leadership capacities, both in the US and abroad, working for an international organization specializing in the design, development, and manufacture of medical devices. As Director of Research and Development, I was responsible for managing the product pipeline, leading project teams, handling budgetary and staffing issues, and overseeing the general operations of a satellite facility. These various experiences ultimately prepared me to participate in classroom discussions and make connections between course content and practical applications in business, initially as a student and subsequently as an instructor. My time spent overseas has equally allowed me to understand alternative perspectives and relate well to others, which are more important than ever in light of globalization and pressing world concerns.

As a life-long learner, I have expanded my wealth of knowledge through the various challenges and responsibilities offered to me over the years. In my current role as Assistant Professor, I hope to impart much of what I experienced—and continue to learn—to students, encouraging and challenging them to reach beyond mediocrity, and reinforcing the need for them to also become life-long learners.

ALINA M. WAITE, PHD
Assistant Professor, Department of Human Resource Development and Performance Technologies, College of Technology TC 302-G, Indiana State University, Terre Haute, IN 47809. Phone: 812.237.3382. Fax: 812.237.2655.
Alina.Waite@indstate.edu

SEE THE BIGGER PICTURE

Everyone can benefit from an overview, seeing where new experiences will fit into what they already know and where they want to go, what challenges lie ahead and what new thinking may be needed. Understanding the benefits of exploration, stretching, and self-reflection can help people take the risks they need to move out of old and comfortable but stale patterns and experience new possibilities, new insights, and new creative energies, often bonding with others in deeper, more meaningful, and more enjoyable ways.

Tip 1. Consider more experiential learning

In *Academically Adrift*, their provocative critique of higher education in the US, Arum and Roksa (2011, 98) identify a striking shift in student time on campus spent away from studies and into work, friends, and recreation.

> In addition to attending classes and studying, students are spending time working, volunteering, and participating in college clubs, fraternities, and sororities…A recent study of University of California undergraduates reported that while students spent thirteen hours a week studying, they also spent twelve hours socializing with friends, eleven hours using computers for fun, six hours watching television, six hours exercising, five hours on hobbies, and three hours on other forms of entertainment. Students were thus spending on average 43 hours per week outside the classroom on these activities—that

is, over three times more hours than the time they spent studying…Given that students are spending very little time studying or attending classes, in both absolute and relative terms, we should not be surprised that on average they are not learning much.

Without sacrificing standards, list ways that you could tap the natural draw of experiences outside the formal school or work environment. Identify how hands-on activities energized your own learning in the past and how it could boost engagement in an upcoming presentation.

Tip 2. Explore difficult issues

One arena where experiential learning has critical value is in exploring difficult issues. Too often we are locked into particular positions or blinded to our own prejudices and assumptions. An extended focus on direct experience can unlock new insights. For example, Timpson et al. (2003; 2005) pushed beyond the usual campus celebrations of different cultures to review the published research on handling diversity in the classroom and then drew on their own experiences as well as what others contributed to offer a new synthesis. Following a similar path, Timpson et al. (2006) wanted to bring new thinking to the issue of teaching sustainability, a very complex and contentious concept that is inherently interdisciplinary, even trans-disciplinary. Similarly, Timpson et al. (2009), representing different disciplines and cultures, also came together to share their experiences and expertise in order to create a new synthesis about teaching peace and reconciliation.

Reflect on instances when you were stuck in old, dysfunctional thinking and new experiences allowed you to get to different insights and possibilities. Consider activities that would help others explore new thinking about a difficult issue.

Tip 3. Immerse yourself

One powerful aspect of experiential learning is gaining new advocates as more and more students find ways to serve or study abroad. Whether it is a church group taking teenagers to Central America to help build homes, day care centers, or health clinics, or college students wanting an alternative experience over one of their breaks or to study abroad for an entire semester, experiences in another culture can be challenging, difficult, and life changing, far beyond what academic studies alone can provide. The US Peace Corps prides itself on offering the "toughest job you'll ever love." Note how they describe what they offer in the way of experience.

The Peace Corps traces its roots and mission to 1960, when then Senator John F. Kennedy challenged students at the University of Michigan to serve their country in the cause of peace by living and working in developing countries. From that inspiration grew an agency of the federal government devoted to world peace and friendship.

Since that time, 200,000+ Peace Corps volunteers have served in 139 host countries to work on issues ranging from AIDS education to information technology and environmental preservation.

Today's Peace Corps is more vital than ever, working in emerging and essential areas such as information technology and business development, and contributing to the President's Emergency Plan for AIDS Relief. Peace Corps volunteers continue to help countless individuals who want to build a better life for themselves, their children, and their communities. (US Peace Corps nd.)

Reflect on those difficult experiences that have taught you the most. List some ideas, both short- and long-term, that could offer something similar for groups with whom you work.

Tip 4. Engage, connect, and construct

In experiential education, learning is an active and constructive process where knowledge is constructed by the interaction of the learner directly with the phenomena. The facilitator works to engage participants with the knowledge/experience and with each other (figure 1).

Here the learner (student) is an active participant whose individual life experiences, loves, passions, biases, and prejudices are intimately involved in the learning process. Together groups of students can create vibrant learning communities.

For an upcoming session, diagram the ways in which you would like to see the flow of information, ideas, and power happen. How can this model help you understand a particularly meaningful experience in the past?

Tip 5. Define your philosophy of teaching

Writing down your philosophy of teaching can be a valuable exercise in critical reflection and values clarification. This can be a catalyst for you to check in with beliefs and understandings that you have created over time and to see where experiential learning could fit. This can also serve as an opportunity to ask yourself about any assumptions that you may have. Consider these questions:

- How do I see the student?
  - Is the student active or passive?
  - What assets and liabilities does the student bring?

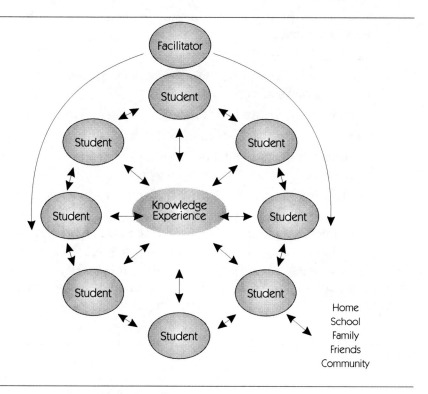

Figure 1: Facilitator engages participants

- Is it my job to motivate the student?
- What is knowledge?
- Does knowledge exist to be discovered, or do we create knowledge?
- What is the nature of knowledge in my discipline?
- Is it my job to impart knowledge, or facilitate the student's interaction with it?
- Is knowledge static or dynamic; for example, does history change depending on the historian's perspective?
- What is my role as an instructor (Palmer 1998)?
- Where do I sit in the "power paradigm" in relation to knowledge and the student?
- What are my responsibilities and what are the student's responsibilities?
- What is my philosophical orientation (behavioral, constructivist, cognitive)?
- How did I get to this orientation?
- Did it emerge from personal experiences or was it adopted from external sources?
- Does it still fit for students today?
- How do I know that I am an effective facilitator?
- How am I evaluated; and more importantly, is this evaluation a valid representation of my teaching?
- Do I invite constructive criticism from my students, peers, and experts?
- Am I open to integrating this feedback into my instruction?

By developing your philosophy of teaching *and keeping it updated,* you will engage in critical reflection about yourself as a facilitator of learning and as a leader. You will also be open to seeing where you could grow, what new experiences you might need.

Ask yourself these questions and write a draft of your philosophy of teaching.

LEARN ABOUT UNDERLYING CONCEPTS

Your understanding of experiential learning will increase with some knowledge of the underlying principles that support active and interactive learning, i.e., the nature of the concepts that can build through various activities, the insights that can emerge through discovery, how developmental psychologists see our abilities to understand and move from the concrete to the abstract, how the brain works, and more.

Tip 6. Frame the activity

When introducing an activity or lesson to a group we often frame the activity—that is, we "set the scene." This helps people connect with the context and the intent of the activity. This also allows them to prepare physically, emotionally, and mentally for the challenges ahead. Often when scaffolding an experience—creating successively more challenging activities—the lessons learned from a previous activity during debriefing can be transferred to a new challenge through thoughtful "framing." The creation of a metaphoric frame that gains meaning and importance as people progress through the experience can increase the potential for transfer to new experiences and insights (Priest and Gass 2005).

For example, consider a group that has just had mixed success in designing a project to help feed homeless people. When they debriefed the project, they discovered that they had very different ideas about the final product, but had not communicated those clearly with each other. Some "framing" would have helped. Imagine that you are facilitating a new project that will develop reading resources for at risk youth. When framing the goals and outcomes for this project, the group decides to create a motto: "All voices heard—all ideas explored." By creating this simple slogan they have not only transferred their learning from the previous activity, but also projected that learning into a vision for the new project.

Consider how you will frame your next project and how you might integrate a theme, a metaphor, or some other tool to help give a frame to the learning.

Tip 7. Scaffold the experience

Scaffolding a learning experience is similar to training wheels on a bike (Bruner 1975). If simply given the bike without training wheels, a child's learning curve can be steep and dangerous. By adding a supportive structure, success can come more quickly. As people move toward mastery, the facilitator (or student) removes part or all of the scaffolding.

The support that you offer during the initial learning stages can include:

- Breaking the task into smaller pieces
- Helping people tie new ideas or skills to prior knowledge
- Providing resource material in different forms to engage different learning styles
- Using groups that provide team members immediate assistance
- Outlining steps so that everyone can measure progress toward a goal

The facilitator helps people become self-directed and independent, in part by increasing the level of risk and difficulty with each successive activity.

Use scaffolding when planning your next project or presentation activity.

Tip 8. Choose the learning experience

With a wide range of ideas for instructional lessons and learning activities, how does anyone choose the most effective experience? Consider the following process when designing a session. First go to the big picture (figure 2).

In this diagram you have multiple decision points as you conceptualize, plan, and facilitate a learning experience.

- An *audience analysis* allows you to look at the demographics, opportunities, barriers, and prior learning of individuals and a group.

- The *stakeholder review* ensures that your design is in alignment with the mission and vision for your institution and helps you build a base of support for your planned program (Caffarella 2002).

- An overall *learning goal* drives the direction of your session and the specific outcomes you want to achieve (Objectives).

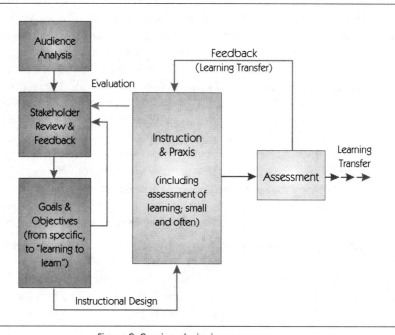

Figure 2: Session designing process

- The actual *learning experience* that you choose (Instruction and Praxis, above) is driven by your findings from the previous steps.

It makes no sense to complete an audience analysis, gather stakeholder input, and develop specific learning outcomes and then randomly choose the experience that you will facilitate—that choice should be informed by the process. In the end your intent—the why of choosing a particular learning experience—needs to be well informed by the data you gather.

The next time you are designing an experiential learning session, create a diagram that represents the flow of working through each of the elements pictured in the diagram above.

Tip 9. Build on previous sessions

Jacqueline McGinty has taught graduate classes on adult education. She writes:

> In classes where I use facilitated dialogue, my students are provided the opportunity to share their life experiences with a small group. Their insights and experiences add a real richness. I try to create a safe learning environment that encourages student participation. I want students to see that I know them and that I value their input. During class discussions I will often make notes about important points that were made and who said them. I also pay attention to what they say about work life, family, and personal experiences. In subsequent classes, I can then include information about them that can help make the material we study more relevant and meaningful. When giving examples in class, I frequently tailor them to what I know about the students. When discussing teaching methods, I will frame my strategies to match the prior experiences of the class.

As a reference for her commitment to including what is meaningful for students, Jackie found this quote from *Tuesdays with Morrie, An Old Man's Reflections on Life's Greatest Lessons:* "Morrie knew better. He saw right to the core of the problem, which was human beings wanting to feel that they mattered" (Albom 1997, 112).

Reflect on times when your experiences, interests, and ideas were included in a lesson by an instructor. Identify ways in which you could incorporate more that is meaningful about the lives of your own students.

Tip 10. Study the art of facilitating experiential learning

In *The Tao of Leadership,* John Heider states that "few leaders realize how much how little will do" (1985, 85). When facilitating experiential activities in the classroom, it can be important for the teacher/facilitator to hold back and allow the group to work. The leader's release of control can result in more meaningful experiences for people as they struggle to complete an activity, discuss it, and make meaning of it for themselves. This might mean that the teacher gives minimal instruction and allows students to grapple with accomplishing the task. It may also mean the facilitator might want to sit back during discussions and allow participants to talk, listen, and question each other. As the instructor becomes less visible, students can move into more active participation. The good group leader knows that by the end of the activity, students should be saying, "We did it ourselves" (Heider 1985, 33).

Reflect on experiences when the teacher, leader, or facilitator allowed the group to work. List ways in which you could "sit back more and let the group work" in an upcoming session.

Tip 11. Embrace risk

By definition, risk to some varying degree is inherent to learning since we stagnate without mistakes, feedback, and correction. That risk, however, can take on many forms. One form is physical—the potential for bodily harm. A second form of risk is emotional or psychological (Brown 1999). This form of risk often goes unnoticed. Having a range of personalities in a group, from those who are risk seekers to those we could consider risk adaptive and others who are risk averse, will challenge any instructor.

Covey (2004) argues that we need to help students take a proactive approach in confronting the challenges they face. As instructors we can help people be more proactive, to reflect, plan, and practice new responses. Otherwise individuals are likely to be reactive and continue old, dysfunctional or counter-productive habits. Typically some form of scaffolding (progressive levels of difficulty or complexity) in designing the learning sequence can be helpful. This allows people to challenge themselves at a "safe" level before moving to a more difficult level.

Risk can add or detract from a learning experience depending on the type, level, and intensity of the risk. As a facilitator you can use risk as a tool to enhance potential outcomes, but you'll need an understanding of the concept and a plan for how to use it.

Identify the levels of physical and emotional risk in a past activity and how scaffolding could have helped your own learning. List ways in which you could introduce risk into an upcoming presentation, session, or activity.

Tip 12. Model what you expect, allow for practice, and solicit feedback

Creating successful experiential learning activities involves understanding a number of important concepts and mastering a range of skills. For example, knowing how important effective communication is for cooperative learning, group leaders can accomplish much by their modeling of best practices. Social work scholar Mona Schatz (2003, 129) makes this case for her own campus teaching.

> Modeling what we expect seems self-explanatory. It really is not. Modeling appreciation for another person may not be something an instructor is used to doing. Saying "thank you for sharing your own ideas and experiences" indicates to students a sense of your genuine regard. Modeling appropriate self-disclosure is also part of modeling what you expect….We can help students by disclosing our own discomforts, ambivalences, and concerns when talking about sensitive topic areas.

The introduction of mastery learning by John Carroll (1963) and Benjamin Bloom and his colleagues (1956; 1973) challenged traditional teaching to go beyond mere coverage and demonstrate its impact on student learning. Central to mastery is practice, whereby students receive feedback about their explorations and trials. As the old adage goes, "less is more" when learning moves beyond memorization and into application, in particular, where experience allows students to use what they study.

As Barbara Davis writes in *Tools for Teaching,* "Frequent, immediate, and specific feedback helps students learn. Focus your comments on one or two items at a time. Constructive criticism and evidence of progress help sustain students' motivation to learn and to struggle onward on a task" (1993, 182). At Charlie Trotter's high end restaurant in Chicago, staff are especially eager to hear about complaints because that is where the greatest learning and improvement are possible. Trotter himself describes it this way: "It's been said before, but a complaint is a gift. We thank our lucky stars that someone took the time to let us know that we have a problem. We can fix a problem, and we can become permanently better at what we do because of the complaint....Failures are worth more than successes. You learn more from those experiences. You work for success, but it's the failures that will help you get to the next success." (Lawler 2001, 152).

Evaluate the modeling you have seen in different experiential settings. Rethink an upcoming event in light of this argument for modeling. Think about your own learning with respect to the value of practice and feedback. How could you redesign an upcoming lesson or presentation to include opportunities and feedback? Make a list of your own "failures," as well as what you've seen at work or in other settings. What useful feedback do those "failures" offer?

Tip 13. Define your role

As the instructor or presenter, it is important for you to be clear about your role. Will you be a participant, a leader, or both? If you ask students to share a tender moment from childhood, will you also share? Why or why not? How would your sharing support the course goals and objectives? As Timpson writes: "Teaching and learning are shared responsibilities. Instructors need to bring expertise, preparation, enthusiasm, creativity, and a variety of skills to facilitate learning. Students need to bring a motivation to learn, their intelligence, and creativity, their own experiences, a willingness to help, and support others as well as some understanding about what is required for learning in a group context" (2002, 47).

Reflect on a previous group experience in which the leader did or did not join in as a participant. What was the impact? Rethink an upcoming activity with respect to your involvement as the leader.

Tip 14. Understand learning transfer

Learning transfer is an area of study that focuses on ensuring that what happens in the classroom, training room, or other formal environment can be transferred to people's lives or work. In experiential learning this can also be referred to as *transference*. While there is debate as to exactly when learning transfer happens (often at the end of the experience), being conscious of its potential in the beginning stages of instructional design is critical (Kaminski, Foley, and Kaiser 2013).

For example, you should have learning transfer in mind when developing the outcomes for every lesson or session. Ask yourself not only what specific outcomes you want people to achieve, but also what skills and abilities they will need. If your goal is to have them master skill set A in the context of conditions B to produce C, what happens when the B at work does not look exactly like the B that you described in training? What other skills can be introduced and integrated so that people can critically analyze the B that they face at work or in life and find a useful way forward? You might have people role play to work through various cases or problems and then reflect on lessons learned. Will they be able to extend those insights into their own lives?

Do your stated outcomes for a specific session address learning transfer?

Tip 15. Have intentional learning outcomes

A learning goal defines the overall intended outcome and can be written as a series of statements that describe what the learner will be able to do. Start with a sentence stem like the following: "By completing the activity, the learner will…" This is followed by a verb with "measurable" qualities such as tell, express, interpret, examine, formulate, assess. Then, a product or outcome is defined, for example, "After the activity or experience, the learner will assess its impact on knowledge acquired, feelings…" So a sample learning outcome might look as follows: "After sexual harassment training, the learner will recognize when specific behaviors are appropriate or inappropriate in the work place." The verb is key to the accuracy of measuring the outcome. A great resource for determining these verbs is Bloom et al.'s *Taxonomy of Educational Objectives* (1956).

Writing outcomes of this sort demands that you consider the progression your students are making toward mastery. The outcomes should be explicit enough that people know what they need to do, what feedback they can expect, and what the criteria are for moving forward. Or better yet, you can co-create the outcomes with students so that they have both clarity and ownership about what is expected.

_____

Rethink a previous experience in light of this explanation of outcomes. What was expected? What could have been clarified? Measured?

Tip 16. Develop your own learning cycle

Learning cycles are models that can help guide your planning and facilitation. For example, David Kolb's (1984) learning cycle (concrete experience to reflective observation to abstract conceptualization to active experimentation) has been foundational for many texts in adult education and training. But these are generalized concepts and can lack the specificity your students may need for a particular context. So consider creating your own learning cycle. You can take the best from the Kolb model and integrate the uniqueness of your group, the environment in which you work, and the specific learning outcomes you have in mind, to create a cycle or process that best serves your needs.

Here are some questions to consider:

- What are some of the underlying assumptions and experiences of your group?
- Do you want to focus on the process, the end product, or both?
- How much active participation will you expect?
- How can group members assist and support each other, thus creating a holistic learning community?

_____

Create your own learning cycle and use that model when developing your next lesson.

Tip 17. Celebrate failures

Jacqueline McGinty makes a case for allowing students to learn from their experiences.

As educators, we can direct our classes in many different ways. When designing course projects and assessments, we want to ensure the greatest possibility for students to be successful. We can be clear in our instructions, allow time for students to ask questions, and give them the tools that they will need. Create assignments that allow students to make revisions based on your feedback. However, if you can remove some of the pressure for 'getting it right' or 'earning an A', then you can provide space for students to try out new ideas and take some necessary risks.

In his riveting book and video for *The Last Lecture,* Randy Pausch, knowing that he was dying from cancer, offers the following advice: "Experience is what you get when you didn't get what you wanted. That's an expression I learned when I took a sabbatical at Electronic Arts, the video-game maker. It just stuck with me, and I've ended up repeating it again and again to students. It's a phrase worth considering at every brick wall we encounter, and at every disappointment. It's also a reminder that failure is not just acceptable, it's often essential" (2008, 148).

Identify those experiences that you initially thought were failures, but later proved valuable. List the various ways you could build this kind of experience and insight into an upcoming class or presentation.

Tip 18. Promote divergent thinking

A 1968 study by George Land and Beth Jarman (1992) gave 1,600 3-5 year olds a creativity test used by NASA to measure divergent thinking in engineers and scientists. They then re-tested the same children at 10 years of age and then again at 15 years of age. Their findings were alarming. While 98% of children 3-5 years of age scored at the genius level on the creativity test, only 32% of the same children did so at ages 8-10, and then only 10% did do at 13-15 years of age. Moreover, the researchers gave the same test to a large group of adults over the age of 25 and only 2% of those participants scored at the genius level. One thing these people had in common was that they had all been through the modern educational system.

Divergent thinking is the ability to see many possible answers to a question and to see many possible ways to interpret a question. Sir Ken Robinson, an internationally recognized leader in connecting education, creativity, and innovation, gave a famous TED speech in 2006 on the changing paradigms in these areas. He believes that modern education is depressing divergent thinking and creativity, an essential capacity for divergent thinking. A high IQ alone does not guarantee creativity. Instead, personality traits that promote divergent thinking are more important. Divergent thinking is found among people with personalities that have traits such as nonconformity, curiosity, a willingness to take risks, and persistence (Wade and Tavris 2008). We will need students who are divergent thinkers to confront the issues and solve the problems of the twenty-first century.

Reflect on the various ways in which your own divergent thinking has been nurtured or stifled. List what you could do to promote divergent thinking in an upcoming presentation or activity.

Tip 19. Utilize knowledge of teaching and learning style preferences

Learning styles (auditory, visual, and tactile/kinesthetic) and teaching styles (mastery, discovery, cooperative) can be significant factors in student success. Awareness of these preferences and their interactions can also be important. Celli and Young (2014) advocate having ongoing conversations between students and teachers to promote greater skill at identifying these learning needs and adapting various instructional preferences. The key is to prepare lessons that have both breadth and depth, and then allow students the flexibility to address the same skill in different ways. Experiential learning, in particular, can provide insights into student needs that classroom instruction cannot.

Reflect on a previous experience and how both learning and teaching style preferences played out. Knowing what you know about a class or audience, list what you can do to accommodate these differences in the future.

Tip 20. Walk in their shoes

As a teacher of adults, Jacqueline McGinty understands that there are many things that teachers need to attend to in their classrooms.

I deliver subject matter, provide feedback and assessments, and engage students in the course material. Yet I also know that we as instructors spend much of our lives rooted in our role as experts, paying homage to our own disciplinary paradigms and then presenting our ideas in class. There we see students, but do we ever stop to ask ourselves who they really are and what it might be like to live their lives? How do they see the course content and our teaching style? We often reflect upon ourselves and our own beliefs; how often do we take time to reflect upon the experience of each learner?

McGinty continues:

> In a course that I am teaching I decided to give the students a questionnaire about themselves. I was noticing that in class they often appeared tired or preoccupied. I began to wonder what aspects of their lives outside of class may be affecting their experiences in class. I asked them where they worked and how far they had to drive to get to class? The course is late in the evening and many of the students have another class beforehand. I wondered if they had a chance to eat dinner? Were they full time students? Parents? What else is going on that could impact their learning?

> When I look at my students holistically, I think I can uncover hidden dimensions that allow for greater synthesis and transformation. Reading the answers to the student questionnaires gave me the opportunity to 'walk for a moment in their shoes.' It provided me with valuable perspectives on their realities. It also provided me with an opportunity to look beyond myself and my own experiences. This helped me to see my students more as individuals and less as a sea of people before me. In *Pedagogy of the Oppressed,* Paulo Freire (1970, 182) wrote:

>> Revolutionary leaders commit many errors and miscalculations by not taking into account something so real as the people's view of the world: a view which explicitly and implicitly contains their concerns, their doubts, their hopes, their way of seeing the leaders, their perceptions of themselves and of the oppressors, their religious beliefs (almost always syncretic), their fatalism, their rebellious reactions. None of these elements can be seen separately, for in interaction all of them compose a totality.

List the various ways by which you could better know your students, what interests them, and who they are as individuals.

UNDERSTAND DEVELOPMENTAL PRINCIPLES

Developmental psychologists have clarified the essential connections between touch, taste, sight, and learning—how our experiences as infants, for example, before we have any language, build a foundation for abstract and symbolic thinking. Later in life, too many instructors or group leaders seem to forget this and put excessive reliance on verbal learning. Our memories are so much stronger when we can access some tangible experience with a concept under study.

Tip 21. Understand Piaget and Bruner

Jean Piaget (1952; 1970) made the case for cognitive development, how infants move from *concrete operational thinking*, when infants begin to build their first understanding through a sense of touch, to *formal operational thinking*, when they can begin to use language and abstractions to understand their world.

In *A Study of Thinking*, Jerome Bruner and his colleagues (1967) describe how infants first learn through touch, taste, smell, and sight before they develop their abilities to think with language and abstractions. Instructors and presenters should remember that people of any age will have a much more solid understanding when they have some kind of experiential basis for the abstract concepts that they are trying to learn.

Identify ways in which you can build understanding through hands-on learning experiences. Identify the various ways that you could deepen understanding by tapping into the senses of touch, taste, smell, and sight.

Tip 22. Support self-determination

Independent thinking forms the foundation for intellectual growth, emotional maturity, and democratic citizenship. Yet, in order to maintain classroom control some teachers focus instead on controlling behavior through punishment and reward. According to Kohlberg (1963), a fear of punishment is the lowest form of moral development. Policies, rules, and laws have their place, but students also need to develop their abilities to make decisions on their own.

Reflect on the various rules you were given to follow in school and when you were encouraged to think independently. Rethink an upcoming presentation or assignment and list the ways in which you could promote independent thinking.

Tip 23. Create a tension between the known and the unknown

As a facilitator you are often trying to create new meaning by making a bridge between the known and the unknown. People come to you with their learning histories, their life experiences, and much knowledge (Dewey 1938). If you can create a tension between what they know, areas that are comfortable for them, and what they do not know, areas that often make them uncomfortable, you increase the probability that they will open up to new ways of knowing. If the known and the unknown are similar, learning may happen quickly and seamlessly. On the other hand, if the known and the unknown are so far apart that people struggle to see connections, learning can prove to be very difficult. As the facilitator, you can point out the connections between the known and the unknown so that you get everyone engaged.

Jean Piaget (1952; 1970) described this process in two ways. *Assimilation* occurred when people could integrate new learning into existing schema or thinking. *Accommodation*, in turn, required a change in thinking to incorporate the new concepts. Prejudice is a good example, here. If you believe that girls lack the assertiveness needed to problem solve out-of-doors and you encounter a girl who is very good at it, then she becomes an "exception to the rule"; that is, you *assimilate* (integrate) your experience into what you already believe. If, however, you experience enough of these "exceptions," you could change (or accommodate) your previous assumption and drop that prejudice (figure 3).

The art of facilitation involves your realizing when tension exists and what influence you might have to impact learning. For example, consider your role when you are introducing a game like kick ball. Some people may have played before, others may have played a similar sport like soccer, and some may never have played a game where they kicked a ball. Those who have played before may be ready to jump right in. Those who have played soccer understand the essence of the game, but need to know the rules specific to kick ball. However, those folks who have never kicked a ball before will need a different set of instructions. Someone who is terrified of performing or playing in front of others might be traumatized by it all!

A master facilitator realizes that people in a group will often be at different developmental levels and will need a safe and engaging environment that is inviting to all, regardless of skill or experience level. While kick ball is relatively straightforward, imagine what it would require to experience, explore, and process constructs like racism, power, and privilege. The tensions would be much more complex and challenging to facilitate. Freire (1970) argued that people need to engage their own oppression in order to break that cycle. Helping people move from the known to the unknown is one way to do this. As a facilitator you can learn to play with this tension between the known and the unknown.

Reflect on the tensions you have experienced between the known and the unknown, what you were able to learn, and what could have been better. For an upcoming experience, think through these tensions and adapt your plans accordingly. Identify what you will do differently.

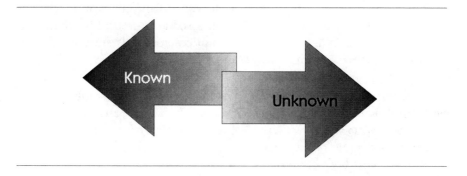

Figure 3: Tension between the known and unknown

KNOW HOW THE BRAIN INTERPRETS EXPERIENCE

We know more and more about how the brain works, what engages the mind on a physiological level, and what the implications are for teachers and group leaders. We know, for example, how experiences will typically engage the brain differently than classroom instruction.

Tip 24. Engage the brain

In *Igniting Student Potential,* Gunn, Richburg, and Smilkstein draw connections between emerging data from neuroscientists that support active, interactive, and experiential learning. Yet traditional instruction and assessment push instructors into a focus on memorized or *surface* learning. While note-taking during a presentation requires a degree of active involvement, if the goal is only to memorize and recall for some later test then we greatly underestimate what will fully engage the brain. "We do rote learning also by our activities. However, for rote learning, the activity is usually just copying and/or memorizing. A neural network for rote-learned material is small; and our understanding is superficial, our knowledge and skill limited" (2007, 56).

While some memorized knowledge is useful for recall in those moments when most needed, we can usually find the time to search for answers, especially now that technology makes so much accessible so quickly. In order to promote more active involvement among your students, rethink an upcoming presentation and focus more on what you will ask of those attending to do as follow-up to the questions you raise. Make a list.

Tip 25. Know how experiences can stimulate the growth of neural networks

Gunn, Richburg, and Smilkstein describe the physiological benefits of rich, complex, and engaging experiences. "As a specific network grows from our experiences, the more we know about, understand, and can do with that specific object of learning—and the more in-depth, complex, refined, and sophisticated our knowledge and understanding become for that object of learning" (2007, 55).

After planning for experiential learning, challenge yourself to design assignments or projects that require complex thinking and push for deeper understanding. Worry less about knowledge level assessment and think more about a scoring rubric that reflects critical and creative thinking.

Tip 26. Tap into the natural learning process

As we learn more about the basic functioning of the brain, we see more of the value of experiential learning. Gunn, Richburg, and Smilkstein report how learning is hard-wired. The more that students are "actively engaged in learning by their natural learning process—doing inquiry-based, problem-solving, pattern-seeking, student-centered, thought-provoking activities, which they are born to do and derive pleasure from doing—the more they are motivated to continue learning about that particular object or learning, that unexpectedly pleasing theme or focus" (2007, 41).

Reflect on a recent memorable experience. What aspects were inquiry-based? Problem-solving? Student- (or person-) centered? Thought-provoking? Describe a future activity with these in mind.

Tip 27. Tap into multiple intelligences

Among the many arguments for experiential learning is the writing of Howard Gardner (1983; 1999; 2000) on multiple intelligences. Especially popular among elementary and secondary school teachers, this work describes eight "intelligences." The *linguistic* and *logical-mathematical* are the two that schools typically emphasize and test. However, there are six others that Gardner insists are essential to what makes us human and of these, several are essential to experiential learning. *Bodily-kinesthetic* intelligence is the most obvious. However, *intrapersonal* intelligence or self-awareness is also essential to experiential learning as is *interpersonal* intelligence or how individuals interrelate with others. *Naturalistic* intelligence reflects those talents that connect us to the environment. Finally, *existential* or *spiritual* intelligence permits us to consider those larger metaphysical questions of meaning.

Compared to traditional classroom instruction, experiential learning offers us a broader perspective of human abilities. As Gardner describes it: "Deviating from established wisdom, I do not believe that there is a single best representation for any core idea or set of ideas. The notion of such a representation is an illusion, usually derived from a particular history of contact with a concept—how the teacher has first encountered it, or how it was initially presented or written about" (1983, 202). The challenge for all teachers, then, is to go beyond how they learned in school and explore the many varied ways that ideas can be presented, studied, experienced, and explored.

Reflect on the "intelligences" that underlie learning in your own experience. List the various ways you could tap into a "broader" perspective for an upcoming presentation.

Tip 28. Use the five senses

Activities allow people to learn by engaging all their senses. In *Leadership and the New Science,* Meg Wheatley makes this claim: "Information provides true nourishment; it enables people to do their jobs responsibly and well" (2001, 107). Experience offers additional insights beyond what can occur in classrooms.

Think back to those experiences that fully engaged your senses while providing the "nourishment" you needed. Rethink an upcoming event and list how a multisensory experience might add real value. Consider the visuals you could add, in particular, if there are relevant film clips that illustrate certain points.

RETHINK CLASSROOM INSTRUCTION

Many teachers and group leaders fall into very conventional habits with "talk and chalk" lessons, thinking that the classroom restrains them from using other approaches. Experiential learning—from individual activities at their desks to what students can do in small groups to projects in and around the building and beyond—can energize instruction and deepen learning.

Tip 29. Commit to democratic classrooms

In *Democratic Schools*, James Beane and Michael Apple throw down the gauntlet and call for more inquiry-based education. In a student-centered environment, they argue, students come with a wealth of knowledge. In a "democratic school it is true that all of those directly involved in the school, including young people, have the right to participate in the process of decision making" (1995, 9). Classroom experiences are typically more meaningful when student ideas and motivations are considered. The best teachers find ways to engage students with the curriculum or content standards that need to be addressed. A commitment to a democratic classroom can help support a two-way flow of communication. Everyone benefits when future citizens are independent, confident learners who know how to investigate issues, problems, and competing claims.

Reflect on the ways in which you were involved as a student in decisions about classroom activities in the past. List ways in which you could promote greater ownership and a shared commitment to learning in an upcoming activity or presentation.

Tip 30. Introduce the elephant in the room

Your awareness about problems that could undermine a group's success is always important. Experience can tell you that some agendas may be hidden, for example. In his national bestseller *The Last Lecture*, Randy Pausch (2008) wrote about his diagnosis of terminal cancer and the process he underwent to get up on stage for a final and, he hoped, inspirational talk. In the moments before he was to begin, he continued to fumble with the stories he wanted to share, which slides to keep or discard. For some members of the audience, this would be the last time they would see him alive. Pausch described his ongoing internal dialogue about his own fear, wondering how the audience members would receive him and if some would be preoccupied with his condition. In a moment of brutal honesty, he chose to open his lecture by addressing what he sensed everyone, himself included, was thinking—the details of his diagnosis. He referred to this tension as the "elephant in the room." Rather than ignoring the obvious, Pausch stated it at the outset, allowing everyone to move beyond the barriers of social self-consciousness into openness about the very authentic experience they were about to.

Deanna Leone, a Student Affairs professional at a large public research university, often discovers this same effect. "When I teach and I'm honest about naming what is happening in the room, I have found that my students will usually move into a more genuine learning moment with me rather than ignoring it or wondering if anyone else notices. Students will often open up and be more willing to talk about their thoughts, feelings, and reactions to the topic rather than stay closed off and use safer, shallower responses."

Consider a time when you felt relieved because someone said what you were thinking when you did not want to be the first to say it. In that moment, did the conversation become deeper or more meaningful because you could focus on what was being said rather than what was not being named? Identify ways in which upcoming discussions offer you opportunities to name the "elephant in the room" and move toward a more honest exchange of ideas and reactions.

LEARNING OUTSIDE CLASSROOMS

In our memories of school, the details that often stick are the sights and sounds, the extracurricular, our friends, and those moments that are transcendent—our shining moments as well as all those embarrassments that make us cringe. These contexts, often outside the classroom, provide untapped resources for active and interactive learning.

Tip 31. Find your own special place

Lisa Pitot is an experienced middle school science teacher who has also worked at Colorado State University. She writes: "In terms of place-based education, we have to ask what exactly is *place*? Place-based educators like van Eijck and Roth know that place is more than just a location, that place encompasses space and time. Individuals and people come to be defined by place as much as place comes to be defined by individuals and people…It is from ages 10-11 that we get our grounding. Taking the time to return to our roots can help us get re-grounded."

Respond to the following: Think about a special place when you were young. Is it inside or outside? What stands out? What do you see? Hear? Smell? After thinking about it for a while, draw a map of your special place. After completing your map, write down your observations. What emotions, if any, came up? Take time to share and discuss your map with others. Reflect on whether this exercise was easy or hard. Were your memories fact-based, emotional, or both? Identify a special place in your life today. What connections are there with your special childhood place? How can your special places inspire you to help students find and tap those places that are special to them?

Tip 32. Find your place and dig in

In his provocative book, *Earth in Mind,* David Orr challenges every-one to wake up to what is happening to our environment and the life support systems that sustain us all.

> We are caught in the paradox that we cannot save the world without saving particular places. But neither can we save our places without national and global policies that limit predatory capital and that allow people to build resilient communities, to conserve cultural and biological diversity, and to reserve eco-logical integrities. Without waiting for national governments to act, there is a lot that can be done to equip people to find their place and dig in. (2004, 170)

Where is your "place"? List what you need to "dig in" and make a difference? How can you connect your subject matter to what is happening to the environment?

Tip 33. Investigate campus and community ecology and assign or encourage action projects

We really do not have to go far afield to find worthwhile projects for meaningful experiential learning. Much can be studied and changed in our own backyards, communities, businesses, schools, colleges, and uni-versities. In *147 Tips for Teaching Sustainability: Connecting the Envi-ronment, the Economy and Society,* Timpson et al., describe what is possible on campus when instructors tap into resources on experiential learning.

> With its emphasis on promoting sustainability in higher educa-tion, Second Nature has developed a treasure chest of materials for teaching, curriculum, institutional policy, and more...The National Wildlife Federation's work on campus ecology has re-sulted in a series of Yearbooks that describe what various col-leges and universities have accomplished. (2006, 87)

Identify local areas of interest that could engage the interests and imaginations of students or other audiences. List a range of ideas for experiential learning.

Tip 34. Be outside and do nothing

Lisa Pitot has used "solo sits" to raise awareness about the environment. She likes to set the stage with a provocative reference. One from David Orr (2004) defines "biophilia" as that connection with the rest of life that is innate for humans.

Pitot writes:

> Experiential educators who are themselves quite comfortable with the above references must recognize that others may not agree. Teachers and students may have their own reasons or issues for preferring to be inside. It is important that we check out all assumptions before embarking on trips outside of the classroom. In addition, we can all learn how to challenge assumptions in light of new ideas, but to do so with respect and sensitivity. Any discomfort that comes with a challenge can also be a catalyst for important growth and learning.

Once a group is comfortable with what to expect, the next step is to be outside and do nothing.

The instructions for solo sits are simple: Find a place outside where you are at least an arm's length (in all directions) from another person. Sit down and relax; do nothing, say nothing. Try not to think of anything; if thoughts drift into your mind, notice them and let them go.

Pitot writes:

> What sounds simple may in actuality be more difficult. In my own experience practicing solo sits with teachers was a breeze. After a hectic day teachers welcomed the quiet solo time to recharge, even if it was only for ten minutes. As a help, I often shared some of the challenges, e.g., a busy mind, too much to do. Teachers in turn have shared their experiences with doing solo sits with their students. They all had a similar story to tell, usually beginning with a catastrophe the first time they tried it. Their students would exclaim that "this is boring" or ask "what do you want us to do?" Many were unable to sit still. In time, though, teachers would invariably agree that the lamenting would cease and students would begin to come in and beg for a "solo sit." Even so, teachers said that they had to limit these "solo sits" to twice a week, out of concern that they would get in trouble with administrators for "doing nothing."

Commit to trying solo sits for yourself and your students.

Tip 35. Bring the classroom outside

Lisa Pitot has made good use of the Promise of Place website, a project of the Center for Place-Based Learning and Community Engagement. (See http://www.promiseofplace.org/) "It is a useful resource for background information, research studies, and curriculum ideas for place-based education. In terms of addressing common barriers to bringing the classroom outside, they suggest the following: 1) entice (challenge?) people outside; 2) streamline logistics for getting kids outside; 3) celebrate how invigorating the outside can be, even in cold months; 4) simplify and economize transportation needs; 5) develop projects and units where nature and culture blend."

Pitot also reminds us that we will need to keep in mind the characteristics of a positive classroom climate, even when we are outside. (See Timpson 2002). We can focus on the relationship between student morale and productivity, the intellectual excitement of our lessons and the rapport we want to build. We can also emphasize trust and the place for Maslow's hierarchy of needs: Physiological, safety, love, and belonging; self-esteem; and self-actualization. First and foremost, however, in order for any lesson outside to be productive, students will need to be reminded about proper behavior. Many students equate being outside with recess.

Plan for bringing a group outside for a period of time, whether it would be for a solo sit, an hour class period, or a whole day, or more. However, know that it is important to prepare and think of the "outdoor" classroom—including the entire community or region—in the same way you would prepare the regular classroom environment.

Tip 36. Use a continuum

Lisa Pitot knows firsthand about the pressures on classroom teachers at every level:

> Many of us might be thinking that place-based education is a great idea, but schedules are already bursting at the seams and demands on every teacher's time are enormous. Before saying "I can't do it," remember that developing and implementing

place-based learning projects either at a school and/or within the community takes time, patience, and a large dollop of creativity. There is also the deadening reality of inertia—that we will continue to do what is easy, comfortable. Csikszenthmihalyi's *Flow* (1990) is relevant here, as it concerns the invigorating benefits of accepting new challenges. Know that place-based learning projects can be thought of along a continuum. Some projects will not contain every feature, nor will they be at the far end of the continuum as *the most* place-based. For example, a project may range from a broad overview of factual or procedural knowledge to a deep exploration of important concepts, from a required service learning component that connects the classroom and the community to a project that is purely academic.

Rethink an upcoming course and list ways in which you could implement some aspect of service learning. When embarking on a place-based learning project, remember the old saying, "What's the best way to eat an elephant? One bite at a time!"

Tip 37. Engage the world and take action

In *Last Child in the Woods,* Richard Louv recognizes the challenges we face in unhooking young people from the addictive attractions of television, video games, computers, and social networking, in particular, and reconnecting them to the natural world.

> No list of nature activities and community actions can be complete, but here are a few suggestions.... Parents, grandparents, and other relatives are the first responders, but they cannot resolve society's nature-deficit disorder by themselves. Educators, health care professionals, policy-makers, business people, urban designers—all must lend a hand. Many of the activities presented here are adult-supervised (up close or at a distance). However, the most important goal is for our children, in their everyday lives, to experience joy and wonder, sometimes in solitude—for them to create their own nature experiences and, as they grow up, to expand the boundaries of their exploration. (2008, 359)

Identify areas that you could explore and take action. Look through the 100 "Actions we can take" at the end of Louv's book for ideas and sources that could work for you. Make a list of what you will try.

Tip 38. Utilize hands-on experiences in nature

Richard Louv (2008) argues for a radical reform of current educational values and practices that will embrace much more of the natural world as an essential part of the curriculum.

> If educators are to help heal the broken bond between the young and the natural world, they and the rest of us must confront the unintended educational consequences of an overly abstract science education: ecophobia and the death of natural history studies. Equally important, the wave of test-based education reform that became dominant in the late 1990s leaves little room for hands-on experience in nature. Although some pioneering educators are sailing against the wind, participating in an international effort to stimulate the growth of nature education in and outside classrooms…many educational institutions and current educational trends are, in fact, part of the problem. (135)

Identify areas in your own schooling where hands-on experiences in nature would have added value to your learning. Plan a presentation that incorporates learning from nature.

Tip 39. Consider the spiritual dimension

In his best-selling call for action to counter the "nature-deficit disorder" that has appeared among young people in the US and elsewhere, Richard Louv (2008, 304) challenges us to go beyond the usual academic arguments. "The coming decades will be a pivotal time in Western thought and faith. For students, a greater emphasis on the spiritual context could stimulate a renewed sense of awe for the mysteries of nature and science. For the environmental movement, an opportunity arises to appeal to more than the usual constituencies, to go beyond utilitarian arguments to a more spiritual motivation: conservation is, at its core, a spiritual act."

Evaluate your thoughts about the environment and conservation. However you want to define spirituality, is there that dimension in any of your thinking? Where and when can you go beyond the "usual constituencies" and "utilitarian arguments?" Have your students write about the connections they see between their own spiritual path and the environment.

Tip 40. Ask yourself: Is this place holy?

Science teacher and consultant Lisa Pitot likes to provoke a deeper conversation about place by referencing Wes Jackson (1994) and his insistence that *either all places are holy, or none of them are.* She writes: "When I shared this with adult learners, the word 'holy' was instantly challenged. In the discussion that ensued, we explored individual meanings of the word 'holy' and almost everyone was okay with that, but not with any general 'truth'."

Consider the following meditation: Find a place to be by yourself. Get centered within your body and become aware of your breath. Your eyes may be open or closed, whichever is more comfortable for you. Begin to connect with this place. What could make this place feel holy to you? Take another deep breath and relax your mind as you exhale. Close your eyes if they are not already closed and place yourself in the midst of your everyday environment, where you spend the majority of your time. It might be your classroom, your car or your kitchen—whatever comes to mind, just mentally place yourself there for this moment. Breathe in this place. Breathe out this place. Feel the holiness that is here. Hold onto that holiness as you return to the present and when you are ready to open your eyes. Now shift your focus to an "unholy" place and find the holiness that you could not see before.

Being in touch with the holiness of all places can be helpful grounding for embarking on place-based education. Define what is "holy" in the places you inhabit.

DEVELOP GROUP FACILITATION SKILLS

Using experiential learning requires a different set of skills than what many associate with teaching (writing on a board or walking a class through a PowerPoint presentation). There are also all those skills we associate with effective group management (establishing clear goals and objectives, maintaining a group focus, managing the time available and the demands of the place itself, handling the many unpredictables that will invariably surface, communicating effectively, dealing with distractions).

Tip 41. Adopt new names and identities

When anyone enters a new environment there is the opportunity to have a new identity. Too often we are known by our histories, the behaviors, skills, and abilities we have exhibited in the past. Some of these attributes may be positive and helpful, for example, our openness to new experiences. However' some may be limiting, for example, the inhibitions that can restrict our learning. Instead, we can give people the opportunity to re-create themselves in a new situation. At the beginning of a session, you can frame the challenges that lie ahead as opportunities for people to re-create themselves, especially if others in the group do not know them. This invitation can empower people to bring forward the positive traits, skills, and abilities that they want to exhibit. You can also suggest that people can adopt new names or nicknames. New identities may then mean new traits, behaviors, and skills that they can practice (Northouse 2010).

Once in a new environment, ask people what positive traits, behaviors, and skills they want to bring forward and how they could leave the rest behind. For example, your students could pick nicknames for themselves that describe their new identities like "Fearless Fred" or "Self-Sufficient Sarah."

Tip 42. Use your eyes when facilitating and processing experiential activities

It is important for group leaders to make good use of their eyes when facilitating and processing experiential activities (Jacobs, Masson, Harvill, and Schimmel 2009; Whichard and Kees 2006). This means letting your group members know that you won't always be looking at them when they are speaking. Looking away from the speaker helps members speak to each other rather than just to the leader, which can help create a more cohesive group dynamic where communication is directly between members and not directed through the leader. Scanning the group also allows the facilitator(s) to observe others' reactions to what is being said and can facilitate connecting members who may be relating to what is being said, often demonstrated through head nodding. Breaking eye contact with the speaker goes against what many of us have learned about good listening skills, but in a group setting it will be essential to establishing a good group dynamic. Letting your members know up front that you will be scanning the group and why you are doing that will help alleviate discomfort, as well as model a valuable and sophisticated communication skill.

Challenge yourself to scan your group and look away from the person who is speaking in order to become aware of other members' reactions to what is being said and to help members speak to each other rather than just to you and/or through you. Reflect on the experience. Ask the group members for their reactions.

Tip 43. Understand the stages of group development

Tuckman (1965) introduced a group formation model to explain the four stages of group development: forming, storming, norming, and performing (figure 4). In the *forming* stage there is a high degree of dependence on the facilitator since the group is establishing initial roles and relationships and often needs direction. In the *storming* stage, while group members define individual roles and positions, sub-groups of similar beliefs may form and everyone must compromise or otherwise navi-

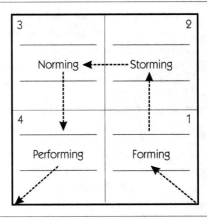

Figure 4: Stages of group development

gate their differences, within their small groups as well as the entire group, in order to move forward. In the *norming* stage agreement and consensus become more important as the group starts functioning more as a whole to solve its problems. In the *performing* stage the team develops a shared vision, a high degree of autonomy, and its own leadership.

A facilitator will want to be conscious of the stage the group is in and align the challenges and tasks accordingly. For example, if you use a high level task to challenge a group that is in the storming stage, you may overshoot their ability at that point in time. But if you adapt the task difficulty to the stages of the group, you can ensure greater success and help build the group's ability to become a healthy, high functioning, and vibrant learning community.

Reflect on your own experiences in groups in the context of these stages of development. As you prepare to facilitate experiential learning, reference these stages to assess a group's collective abilities to meet its challenges and adapt your plans accordingly.

Tip 44. Develop the art of facilitation

I am a teacher—I teach! And often we teach exactly how we were taught, for better or worse. Take a moment to reflect on yourself as a teacher. Are you a traditional teacher or do you tend to use more nontraditional methods of teaching (figure 5)?

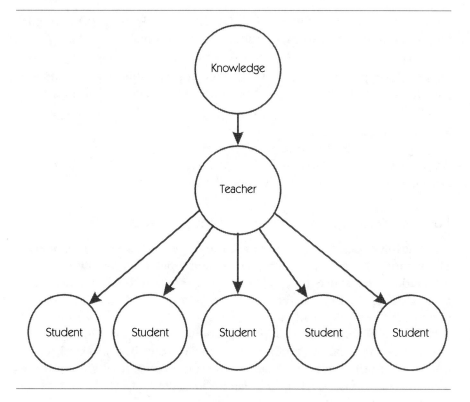

Figure 5: Didactic student/teacher interaction
Source: http://www.flickr.com/photos/justinlincoln/2836568178/

Traditional (Didactic) Education

The Instructor: In didactic instruction, knowledge exists and the instructor transmits that knowledge to the student. This teacher-centered instruction allows the instructor to interpret and filter knowledge as presented to the learner. Palmer (1998) describes this as the objectivist myth of knowing.

The Student: The student in traditional teaching is often referred to as an empty vessel (Freire's Banking Model) or blank slate ("tabula rasa" or "empty table") to be filled with knowledge by the instructor.

Experiential Education

The *Facilitator* in experiential education learning is an active process in which knowledge is constructed by the interaction of the student directly with the phenomena. The facilitator works to engage people with the knowledge experience and with each other.

The Learner: The learner is an active participant in which life experiences (love, passion, bias, and prejudice, for example) emerge and are part of the learning process. Groups of learners can create learning communities.

Reflect on your own experiences of information acquisition versus active co-construction. How could you conduct an upcoming session so as to encourage more co-construction from the experiences that will be shared?

Tip 45. Understand individuals and orient your group

It is important to orient people to an experience before it happens. Think about those times when you had some personal attention and an orientation and those times when you were confused or frustrated. What would have been different if you had known in advance what was expected, both practically and personally, for instance costs, needed supplies, an overview of what the experience would entail, obligations, what fears might arise, whether any participants had physical, emotional, or health concerns? When facing the unknown, anxiety can undermine—or energize—learning. Factor in student strengths and weaknesses as well.

> Positive climate allows us as instructors, whatever our disciplines, to challenge students and maximize learning without fear of emotional meltdowns or unnecessary resistance to change.... Joseph Lowman (1995)... makes reference to climate when he focuses on those factors that drive learning in college. In his view, the best instructors in college combine enthusiasm for their course material with genuine care for students and their learning. (Timpson 2002, 46-47)

Reflect on a past experience that could have been better. Establish ground rules for an upcoming event so that any problems that emerge can be addressed in a timely manner.

Tip 46. Promote progressive interactions

One of the advantages of experiential learning is that it can offer a deeper connection with self, as well as with others. Consider the ground rules that could help participants share information, relate to each other, move through their disagreements, or mesh differing personalities. Michael Fullan's (2005, 46) research on leadership and sustainability offers some useful guidelines:

> Process smart means that progressive interactions exchange information and ideas in ways that foster astute decisions, good solutions, and far-seeing plans. People smart means that progressive interactions foster the cohesiveness of the group, leaving people feeling good about working together and looking forward to doing more together...acknowledging that a certain amount of conflict is productive.

Reflect on those past experiences that were especially important for developing "progressive interactions" with others. What could you do to promote more "people smart" processes?

Tip 47. Distinguish exercises from experiments

Group facilitator and author, Gerald Corey (2013) describes the differences between exercises and experiments stating, that exercises are techniques that are used at times to accomplish something. Experiments on the other hand emerge in the moment of the experience and come out of the here and now experience of the group.

How this translates to experiential education is shown in this example. If I am teaching a lesson on understanding unearned privilege, I may use an exercise such as the "Run for the Wall" activity in which participants begin by holding hands in a line and are directed to step forward or backward from the starting line based on their answers to questions such as, "one or both of my parents graduated from college." Group members are instructed to continue holding hands with those next to them until it becomes literally impossible to stay connected. Conducting and processing this activity can provide a rich source of personal understanding about how we don't all necessarily start with a level playing field.

An experiment on the other hand would perhaps emerge out of a classroom lesson on privilege where some students are having difficulty understanding the "level playing field" as a myth. Students with surnames beginning with letters A-M may be asked to close their eyes while the next 5 minutes of a PowerPoint presentation on privilege is shared. Then the experiment could be repeated with students whose names begin with letters N-Z. A discussion would follow looking at how they felt when they were blinded, when they were not blinded, and how this experience relates to other privileges in their lives.

Learning experiences may emerge at the moment from interactions within the group. Look for these possibilities and risk trying some unplanned experiments that could prove very meaningful.

Tip 48. Develop different ways to draw students into group discussions

Teachers and group facilitators often panic when their discussion questions are met with silence from group members. Because of that panic, leaders will often answer their own questions, change the topic, or resort to calling on members. This is a sure-fire way to stifle spontaneous group interactions and reinforce a traditional classroom hierarchy where group members are more likely to talk to the group leader than to each other.

There are several ways to "warm group members up" to be ready to discuss in a larger group. One way is to have students discuss the topic or question in groups of two or three first and perhaps have them write down the key points of their discussion. Another technique is to have individuals write their answers to a prompting question first before having them share in the larger group. Facilitating group discussions is similar to priming an old time water pump—putting some water into the pump before a steady flow of water could come out. Group facilitators can think of themselves as priming the pump of group interaction. Helping group members learn the expectations of talking to each other rather than to the group leader can create a rewarding and more dynamic flow of discussion (Jacobs et al. 2009).

Reflect on how often group discussions end up with group members speaking to and through the leader rather than to each other. Think about the ways in which you might be reinforcing that habit and ways in which you might retrain yourself and your group members to speak to each other.

Tip 49. Create contracts and agreements for ground rules

In a chapter for _Teaching Diversity,_ social work scholar Mona Schatz (2003, 127) describes the benefits of establishing contracts or ground rules for individuals and groups, especially when the topics involve sensitive, complex material and experiential settings change the relationships in groups. "Contracting with students is one way to flatten the academic hierarchy somewhat. A written contract is not necessary, yet working out the needs students have may require some brainstorming. Some consensus-seeking process is important, and restating agreements made is vital."

When have contracts or set ground rules been useful for your own learning? When not? Explore the use of new ground rules for a group with which you work.

DEVELOP TEAMWORK

Every group experience and project contains opportunities for learning about cooperation and communication, the critical and creative thinking that helps teams address their goals and find constructive ways forward. These are essential life skills, what Gardner (1983; 1999; 2000) refers to as "interpersonal intelligence." Dan Goleman (2009) insists that the "emotional intelligence" needed for relating effectively with others can be much more important for success in life than raw brain power and the ability to memorize and recall.

50. Utilize cooperative learning

One way to deepen learning is to effectively employ small groups and allow time for the sharing of ideas. Group members can learn much from the experience of using their knowledge as they work on projects and problems (Johnson and Johnson 1998). However, much research points to the need for well-developed pro-social skills for groups to be really high performing; for example, effective communication, deep listening, empathy, and consensus building.

Identify the ways in which you benefitted from a cooperative experience. How can you rethink an upcoming project and build in more group experiences?

Tip 51. Build community with dialogue groups

Social work scholar Mona Schatz has come to appreciate particular approaches that help people discuss difficult, complex, and sensitive issues. Especially when away from the formal classroom, experiential learning can offer opportunities for participants to share personal aspects about themselves and to raise a range of concerns in the hope of getting useful responses from people they are beginning to trust. Dialogue groups offer another way to structure this kind of sharing.

> Dialogue through group discussion offers opportunities for transformative experiences and valuable networking, both professionally and personally.... Dialogue has been referred to as an experience of shared exploration toward greater understanding, connection, or possibility.... Dialogue does not seek any tangible outcome. Most importantly, ideas, beliefs, and attitudes are not seen as inherently right or wrong. Dialogue groups are used to create a sense of community and wholeness ....The processes of dialogue groups can move members away from competitive ways of being in social interactions and toward more egalitarian and caring relationships. (2003, 127)

Reflect back on those group experiences that have incorporated "dialogue" in groups as described by Schatz. Plan to introduce these guidelines for a future group activity.

Tip 52. Build a learning organization

According to Peter Senge (1990), principles of teaching and learning can also apply to businesses or agencies, and, when successful, amount to what he refers to as the *learning organization*. As an example, at the Burlington (MA) Uno Chicago Grill, the general manager, the assistant general manager, and the bar manager agree that "showing concern for the employees" and "cultivating a sense of belonging" through "constant communication" will "lower turnover," "leave a legacy of learning," and encourage their willingness to teach others, and especially the customers, about the food quality and hospitality improvements. In contrast, Uno's former Regional Vice President Jon Freedman describes the negative, fear-based climate that a previous employer used. "At the start of my first meeting, the company spokesperson said to us, 'Put your right hand on your left shoulder and your left hand on your right shoulder. Now give yourself a hug because that's the only hug you'll get from us. There was no trust from that point on. They even secretly tape recorded one of their staff members on the phone and then replayed it at a public meeting as an example of what not to do!"

How would you grade your own organization on its ability to "learn," to be "aware" and "motivated" to improve?

Tip 53. Push for the tipping point

Experiences can have a multiplier effect as participants share their successes and setbacks and then discuss what they have learned. The settings, the changes, and the challenges often combine to bond a group together through shared experiences—and it can happen quickly. Knowing about Malcolm Gladwell's argument for a "tipping point" can help group leaders take full advantage of their time together.

> These three characteristics—one, contagiousness; two, the fact that little causes can have big effects; and three, that change happens not gradually but at one dramatic moment—are the same principles that define how measles move through grade-school classroom or the flu attacks every winter. Of the three, the third trait—the idea that epidemics can rise or fall in one dramatic moment—is the most important, because it is the principle that makes sense of the first two and that permits the greatest insight into why modern change happens the way it does. The name given to that one dramatic moment in an epidemic when everything can change all at once is the tipping point. (2000, 9)

Bill Timpson took his doctoral capstone class to a mountain retreat center. After the first afternoon of orientation talks, blindfolded "trust walks," and other group problem solving challenges, the second day began with a hike. By noon they had eaten and some of the group turned around, but others wanted to press on to the snow fields two to three hours ahead. Navigating all the water runoff from that spring's thaw, the log bridges in various states of repair and disrepair, the newly fallen trees and limbs made for a tipping point that helped pull the class members together and will be talked about long into the future.

Reflect on those experiences that proved to be "tipping points" for you. Identify strategies for getting a future group to that transformational point.

Tip 54. Help people understand principles of self-organization

Meg Wheatley offers an intellectual argument for understanding the kinds of changes and challenges that emerge from experiences as people try to make sense of what is happening to them and around them.

The more I read about self-organizing systems, the more I marvel at the images of freedom and possibility they evoke. This is a world of independence and interdependence, of processes that resolve so many of the dualisms we created in thought. The seeming paradoxes of order and freedom, of being and becoming, whirl into a new image that is very ancient—the unifying spiral dance of creation. Stasis, balance, equilibrium, these are temporary states. What endures is process—dynamic, adaptive, creative. (2001, 89-90)

Evaluate a recent experience from the perspective of a self-organizing system, that is, an organization that is dynamic, adaptive, and creative. What insights emerge? How can you rethink a future project?

Tip 55. Get the right people on the bus and have them help move in the right direction

Much can be invested in professional development, but having the best teachers or presenters is the first and most important place to begin. For business, we appreciate the recommendation by Jim Collins and his associates in *Good to Great* about hiring the right people and getting them in the right positions. "The good to great leaders began the transformation by first getting the right people on the bus (and the wrong people off the bus) and then figured out where to drive it" (2001, 63). We want to take this one step further, however, and make a claim for a commitment to development as well. Quality recruitment and placement is, we believe, only the beginning. Getting everyone involved in the experience of designing and building a better bus, as well as helping to guide its direction taps into a high level of intelligence, innovation, and energy.

Restaurant General Manager David Frederick thinks about it this way: "We need to find motivated people who can multi-task. I think we should recruit more from the ranks of student athletes who have the ability to handle competing high-level challenges. They are inherently competitive, energetic, and team players. We also need people who are self-reflective, who can direct their own learning." Uno Regional VP Jon Freedman adds: "In sports, teams will attempt to improve with trades, signing free agents or players who have been released and are on the waiver wire, or developing young talent from within. It's the same in our business" (Guidara and Timpson, under development).

Make a list of the "best passengers" on your organization's "bus." Identify ways in which you could involve them more in determining the best design and direction for this "bus." How could you recruit and use more of the right kind of passenger?

BUILD CLIMATE
WITH EXPERIENCE

We know much about the relationship between morale and learning—how trust, for example, is a foundation for risk taking, critical thinking, and creativity. Experiential learning can build that trust, bonding people through shared risk, cooperative problem solving, etc.

Tip 56. Understand the impact of "climate" on learning

Much research on classroom climate identifies the importance of trust, support, mutual respect, open communication, and problem solving for student morale and learning. In *Concepts and Choices for Teaching,* Timpson and Doe describe the physical aspects of a positive classroom environment:

> It matters that our classes meet in rooms that are comfortable for students, providing them with adequate space and good lighting where they can easily hear their instructors. Operable windows are important for fresh air and natural lighting.... Climate knowledge of this sort...impacts the variety of teaching methods that an instructor can employ, while, in turn, varying the teaching methods helps to reduce student boredom.... The underpinnings of classroom climate reach back many years and offer us a number of useful reference points for improvements. (2008, 34-35)

While climate factors work well in formal classrooms, experiential learning often moves out of doors, where the benefits of fresh air, natural lighting, and shared adventure can add much more.

Rethink an upcoming presentation to incorporate more that is experiential. Add some measure of challenge to see if you can boost morale, engagement, and learning. Identify those factors from the research on positive classroom climate that you have seen with experiential learning.

Tip 57. Create classroom community

There are many reasons to put some effort and thought into creating a community that supports learning. You can help people overcome a sense of isolation, encourage them to engage more in the content and the activities, facilitate a deeper learning experience, hopefully increase everyone's intrinsic motivation to learn (without external rewards like points or grades), discourage drop outs, and promote a greater respect for the diversity of all learners (Lui et al. 2007).

Creating a community can help people look to others to support their learning and capture the benefits of active and cooperative learning, and thus some of the "synergy" that is available, where learning in the group is more than the sum of the parts. This will mean a shift away from a preoccupation with pleasing the instructor or getting all their answers right. Trying new approaches and learning from mistakes will require some confidence and risk. When this occurs, when learning is more independent and interdependent, the facilitator can focus more on the quality of learning and trust that the group will rise to the challenge of supporting its individual members. The setting or classroom then represents a more holistic experience, mixing the learning of course content with personal and group development.

Identify instances when you felt that you had a sense of community. What aspects allowed that community to develop? How could you recreate a greater sense of community in your classes, activities, or presentations?

Tip 58. Be worthy of trust

How often do students enter the classroom thinking about trust, especially between them and the teacher? When and how is trust established in the school environment? Ennis and McCauley (2002, 3) insist that "although there may be a tendency to think of trust as a peripheral aspect of the school environment, we contend herein that trust is, or should be, at the centre of the school experience. Trusting relationships appear to be the first step in expanding and extending students' experiences. Trust as a mutual agreement then paves the way for positive outcomes." Establishing and allowing trust to coexist between students and teachers allows for deeper learning to evolve.

Identify times when trust was established in a group and how important it was to you. List what you could do to build more trust into your class or organization.

Tip 59. Trust your experiences

Too often we become captive of the "stories" we tell ourselves, why we can't do this or why that is impossible. Noted Buddhist teacher and writer, Pema Chödrön, encourages us to live fully, to "smile at fear," to go to "those places that scare us," to embrace life in all its rich tapestry, the tough and the easy, the tragic and the fun, all those facets that are essential to the very process of life itself, to the inevitability of death and our own mortality.

> Our greatest obstacles are also our greatest wisdom. In all the unwanted stuff there is something sharp and penetrating; there's great wisdom there. Suppose anger or rage is what we consider our greatest obstacle, or maybe it's addiction and craving. This breeds all kinds of conflict, and tension and stress, but at the same time it has a penetrating quality that cuts through all the confusion and delusion. It's both things at once. When you realize that your greatest defilement is facing you and there seems no way to get out of it because it's so big, the instruction is, let go of the story line, let go of the conversation, and own your feeling completely. Let the words go and return to the essential quality of the underlying stuff. (2001a, 108)

Reflect on those stories you tell yourself that get in the way of experiencing the richness that life has to offer—your anxieties, fears, or ambitions. Identify all those "lessons" that have made you cautious and self-conscious, eager to please your teachers or parents but increasingly unsure of your own abilities or what may be possible.

COMMUNICATE EFFECTIVELY AND PROCESS EXPERIENCES

Experiences can deepen learning with effective communication skills, whether in the form of written journal entries that allow individuals to sort out their reactions, the articulate expressions that allow us to share with others, or the listening, empathy, consensus seeking, and negotiations that underlie successful group projects and teamwork. As important, however, is the realization that debriefing is central to the effectiveness of experiential learning. Teachers and group leaders must create the time and space and climate for participants to share their reactions, learn from each other, and deepen their own understanding.

Tip 60. Use a quote to open or close a session

A quote can be an effective way to frame and transfer learning. A framing quote might provide a metaphor to highlight an intended outcome or how a lesson could transfer to life or work. For example, for people who seem fearful of taking a risk, consider how they might react to the following quote:

> You risked your life, but what else have you ever risked? Have you risked disapproval? Have you ever risked economic security? Have you ever risked a belief? I see nothing particularly

courageous about risking one's life. So you lose it, you go to your hero's heaven and everything is milk and honey 'til the end of time. Right? You get your reward and suffer no earthly consequences. That's not courage. Real courage is risking something that might force you to rethink your thoughts and suffer change and stretch consciousness. Real courage is risking one's clichés. (Tom Robbins, *Another Roadside Attraction*)

Another quote might encourage people to transfer important lessons to their lives or work.

A ship in a harbor is safe, but that is not what ships are built for. (William Shedd, 19th Century Theologian)

This kind of quote could be an excellent "transference metaphor"—or in David Ausubel's (1967) term, an "advance organizer"—for people who have been together for a while, perhaps for a school year or for an extended project, and they are "outward bound" for some new adventure. There are many themes that could be explored here; for example, "we did not learn these ideas or skills to sit idly by" or "it is time to head out for the next challenge" or "you have been great shipmates, but it is time to go and find some new mates for my next voyage." A quote can serve as a foundation to create new metaphors and new meaning.

Consider opening or closing an upcoming session with a quote. What could have framed a previous experience and added valuable meaning?

Tip 61. Use the language of encouragement

"Whenever we make statements about attitudes, we are making predictions about future behavior of people based on our observations of past behavior" (Mager 1997, 13). Encourage students even when they are struggling and you can help build the confidence that underlies all learning, the willingness to explore new ideas, to try different approaches, to learn from mistakes, and to persevere. Alternatively, discouragement can lead to self-defeating or "avoidance behaviors" that are linked to lower academic accomplishment and feelings of low self-efficacy (Urdan et al. 2002, 71). According to Mager (1997, 14), "No matter what we accomplish, or fail to accomplish, with our instruction, we should do no harm to student attitudes toward learning—and attitudes toward what we are teaching." Everyone who teaches can use more of the positive language of encouragement.

Reflect on those experiences you have had where the language of encouragement had a positive impact on your motivation. When was it that you could have used more encouragement? Rethink an upcoming presentation and note places where you will be sure to add words of encouragement.

Tip 62. Ask what your "balloon" would say?

What is the experience of those who attend your classes, meetings, or presentations? How would they describe their time with you? Would it just be the words that you say or will it reflect something more? Parker Palmer (1998) writes: "One student I heard about said she could not describe her good teachers because they differed so greatly, one from another. But she could describe her bad teachers because they were all the same: 'Their words float somewhere in front of their faces, like the balloon speech in cartoons.'... [The best instructors teach from] their hearts...the place where intellect and emotion and spirit and will converge in the human self" (11).

List the kinds of descriptions people would write in the "balloon(s)" about their experiences in your classes, meetings, or presentations. Now list the kinds of comments you would like to receive and what you could do to get more of these.

Tip 63. Make connections

Most people will fragment or organize information into digestible pieces so that they can have better control or understanding (Bohm 1980). Miller (1956) suggested that humans are limited in memory to seven plus or minus two (i.e., five to nine) units or chunks of information. In our need to fragment information—scholars will talk of "reductionism"—we can lose site of the whole, the "big picture." In *The Web of Inclusion*, Sally Helgesen speaks of a way of "conceptualizing our universe that emphasized the inescapable interdependence of all things, and thus affirms the value and importance of every fragment of the greater whole—the 'universal interwovenness.'" In order to preserve the holistic quality of an experience, reflect on the following questions:

• When do you fragment knowledge?

- What is the consequence of losing sight of the whole?
- How can you design and facilitate a learning experience that sustains this "universal interwovenness? (1995, 16)

When we take the time to do this, we can help people see the interconnectedness of reality.

When you next make a presentation, ask yourself if you are doing enough to frame the big picture, the interconnectedness of concepts and meaning.

Tip 64. Continually communicate the goals, objectives, and assignments of the class

Always keep the course goals and objectives in mind and how you can connect the experiences gained with the ideas that you hope will be learned. For every activity that you plan, ask yourself: "How does this support the objectives of the course?" What actually happens, however, will be largely a discovery process and demand some thought, both individually and collectively, to process.

> Discovery learning is designed to engage students as active participants in the pursuit of knowledge, allowing them to confront a puzzle, a problem, or a challenge, and to follow their own lead towards a solution. It has much in common with higher education's research mission. Instead of asking students to demonstrate their mastery of existing facts and theories, we ask them to turn their attention, creativity, and intelligence toward problems and issues that have no known immediate answer or solution. It is in this cauldron of possibilities that students can best begin to think critically and independently. (Timpson 2002, 86)

Reflect on those experiences when you were left unsure of the program's goals and objectives. Contrast these with experiences when you were able to discover connections that did make sense. Rethink an upcoming event and identify places where you could emphasize what you hope everyone will learn.

Tip 65. Tap your passion

A teacher's enthusiasm speaks volumes to students, convincing them that whatever experience they are having, it has value. In *Concepts and Choices for Teaching,* Timpson and Bendel-Simso (1996, 20-21) write:

> Theater people often use the expression 'raising the stakes,' which points to a simple truth about the stage: Unless both actors and audience are committed to a show, it will flop. The same is true for teaching and learning; if students remain uninvolved in the proceedings, even the best prepared class plan may fail. Teachers can 'raise the stakes' in any number of ways, but in every case the key factor is to make sure that students feel the material matters to them. Once their own passion and excitement have been aroused, as well as your own, teaching can be just as exhilarating and just as much fun as theater. In *Mastering the Techniques of Teaching,* Joseph Lowman (1995, 23) insists: "Like other performers, college teachers must above all else convey a strong sense of presence, of highly focused energy....The ability to stimulate strong positive emotions in students separates the competent from the outstanding college teacher.

In the business world, former Uno Regional VP Jon Freedman insisted that "it's about being a professional at work. I had someone working for me as a manager back in 1983, [a woman] who was being beaten by her husband and struggling with a son on drugs. I saw her drive up to work, get out and slam the door, and put on that smile we all loved her for. Whatever else was happening in her life, she always thought of work as 'her time' and the importance for her to come in with the right frame of mind." Regional Manager Kenny Richards added: "A leader with passion has a vision and brings something electric. Staff members are given the choice: get on the bus or get out. People respond to leaders with passion; they'll run through walls" (Guidara and Timpson, under development).

Reflect on a recent experience. Could the leader's passion have made a difference for you? Identify ways that you could use to better express your own passion in your various activities and projects.

Tip 66. Allow for the freedom to participate—or not

We must always remember that each person is unique and that what is good and easy for one may not always be good for another. Experiential learning can be difficult physically, emotionally, mentally, and spiritually for individuals and groups. There is a line, a tipping point, between what is challenging and what may be debilitating. It can be important to allow for people to opt out of an activity or choose a different way to reach a particular goal. Some instructors create ground rules and agreements for communication that allow them to challenge a group while remaining open and sensitive to different needs and limitations. Noted diversity scholar bell hooks (2003) addresses the emotional costs of activities that cross a line: "When education as the practice of freedom is affirmative in schools and colleges, we can move beyond shame to a place of recognition that is humanizing. Shame dehumanizes.... As teachers we can make the classroom a place where we help students come out of shame" (hooks 2003, 103).

Reflect on an experience when you felt pressured to participate. How could that have been handled differently? Rethink an upcoming event. How can you best balance the challenges you want to create with every individual's freedom to opt out?

Tip 67. Make use of Transactional Analysis (TA)

In *Games People Play*, the classic adaptation of Freudian psychoanalytic theory, Eric Berne (1964) describes three "ego states" that have proven both useful and easily accessible for audiences of all ages to better understand communication and enhance self-awareness, essential components for making the most of experiential learning. In place of the "Superego" where Freud saw our conscience, Berne uses "Parent." Where Freud had our rational selves in the "ego," Berne used "Adult." Where Freud used "Id" to describe our emotional selves, Berne used the "Child." After a morning in the cold, wind, and rain on a university ropes course, Bill Timpson's first year honors students were able to use the language of Transactional Analysis to help talk about "what they should do" (Parent), problem solve various obstacles (Adult), and overcome the potentially paralyzing effects of their fears (Child).

Use the TA model to plan for experiential learning and then process what happens. List the insights you have for future presentations.

Tip 68. Use assertiveness to bolster student judgments and actions

In preparing for the University's ropes course, Teaching Assistant Margit Hentschel paired up with one of the first year honors students who was eager to complete the "circuit" of high elements—climbing up to a platform sixty feet up on telephone poles, then walking across a fifty foot series of wooden ladder-like boards connected by ropes, a telephone pole on its side, another fifty foot high wire element with a few ropes hanging down for balance, and two other high wire elements, culminating in a swing down off that initial platform. While her eighteen year old partner was eager to "do it all," Margit knew that it was that last swing element where she would have to step off the platform and free fall forward that was so terrifying for her in the previous semester. In an almost perfect assertive response, Margit would not "submit" to the pressure from her partner to do the swing nor become "aggressive" to overcome her own doubts. Instead Margit said that she would do the circuit up to the very end and then climb down from the platform—honest, direct, and clear.

Alberti and his colleagues (2008) have written extensively about assertiveness training, how people can learn to distinguish between what is aggressive, what is submissive, and what can be defined as assertive. When combined with opportunities to think through conflicts, plan an appropriate response, visualize and practice preferred responses, and then evaluate the results, a very powerful process emerges that can help people begin to address what are often longstanding, dysfunctional habits and worries.

Reflect on an earlier experience to see where the assertiveness model could have helped participants navigate the challenges that they faced. List ways in which you could use these insights to rethink a future activity or project?

Tip 69. Use nonviolent communication

Marshall Rosenberg has created a system for effective communication that would work well for supporting experiential learning. In his book, *Nonviolent Communication,* he describes the four core elements.

First, we *observe* what is actually happening in a situation: what are we observing others saying or doing that is either enriching or not enriching our life? The trick is to be able to articulate this observation without introducing any judgment or evaluation—to simply say what people are doing that we either like or don't like. Next we state how we *feel* when we observe this action: are we hurt, scared, joyful, amused, irritated? And [third,] we say what *needs* of ours are connected to the feelings we have identified…. [Then, we] follow immediately with the fourth component—a very *specific request*…. This fourth component addresses what we are wanting from the other person that would enrich our lives or make life more wonderful for us. (2002, 6)

When Bill Timpson took his doctoral class to a mountain retreat center for a three day capstone course, a debriefing session the following day revealed a concern that had been simmering and needed to be addressed. A Latina said it this way: "When the group took off on its hike *(observation)*, I felt alienated *(feeling)* because I don't have much experience hiking and most of you do. I want *(need)* to be included in this group. What I would like *(request)* is that in the future we talk through a plan like this in advance, share recommendations about clothing and shoes, and set some ground rules for participation. I want to extend our respect for diversity to this kind of experiential learning."

Identify those aspects of nonviolent communication that were used in one of your past experiences. What can you include in an upcoming program?

Tip 70. View criticism as an act of love

Difficult conversations can be used as a way to address areas of needed growth and learning when approached with compassion and love (Stone, Patton, and Heen 2010). While often viewed as negative, criticism can also serve as an act of love, building and strengthening relationships or guiding individual growth. Within the context of teaching and learning, a willingness to approach a difficult conversation about an individual's need for improvement can create an opportunity to share criticism in a meaningful, constructive, and loving way. If the motivation to offer criticism comes from this place of investment in the growth of another individual, rather than from a place of power, anger, or judgment, then both learning and relationships can flourish.

Identify times in your own life when a criticism you received was difficult to hear, and yet very meaningful in your growth because it came from a person who cared about you personally or professionally? List the ways in which this insight could help you rethink your communication with others in the future?

Tip 71. Recognize that you can't know it all

Because there are so many variables that defy easy control—conditions, individual and group focus, impact, and more—instructors are often nervous about experiential learning. Many struggle to cover all the material in their courses anyway and often worry about liability issues when they do think about taking students outside the classroom. There is also a great deal of pressure on teachers as "experts" to have all the answers. Moreover, many teachers feel consumed by the idea that they must "know it all" in their content areas. Using inquiry-based approaches has the additional threat of allowing questions outside the expertise of the instructor.

In *Nonviolent Communication,* Marshal Rosenberg (2002, 121) makes a case for honest ignorance as a model for building empathy as fallible humans: "situations where we are the most reluctant to express vulnerability are often those where we want to maintain a 'tough image' for fear of losing authority and control." By admitting to what we don't know about a topic, we can model something important for our students. We also develop empathy with the challenges of learning new and complex material that defy simple answers.

Reflect on those moments when you were in a group and at a loss about finding a suitable answer. How could you have rewritten that "script"? What can you do differently in the future?

Tip 72. Know that experiential learning is served better by dialogue than debate

Debate is a common mode of discourse in academic settings. The experiential classroom, however, can be better served through the techniques of dialogue. In her book, *From Debate to Dialogue: Using the Understanding Process to Transform Our Conversations,* Deborah Flick (1998) discusses the primary differences between a culture of debate and a culture of dialogue. In dialogue, one listens for understanding, rather than listening for errors in logic, and the emphasis is on understanding the other, rather than being right or wrong. According to Flick, during the dialogue process "the need to agree with each other becomes less important" and that from a place of understanding each other, new possibilities and ways of thinking may emerge (44). During the processing of experiential activities, it will be important to help people learn and incorporate the dialogue process to avoid devolving into debate. Flick recommends using sentence starters such as, "Help me understand," "Say more about that," and "Tell me more" as ways to facilitate the dialogue process.

When facilitating experiential learning and the follow-up processing discussions, you can begin to foster a culture of understanding and creative exploration with your participants by modeling the dialogue process using the words, "Tell me more."

Tip 73. Process activities

The processing of experiential activities is as important as the activity itself (Jacobs et al. 2009). Know that creating good, open-ended processing questions is an art. There are three basic levels of questions used for processing activities.

- The first level of questioning is at the *level of experience*. Questions at this level would include: What happened? What did you notice or experience? What did you feel?

- The second level of questioning is at the level of *interpretation or insight*. Questions at this level might include: How was your experience during that activity similar or different from other experiences in your life? What did you realize during that activity that might relate to other areas of your life? What did you learn about yourself?

- The third level of questioning is at the level of *application*. Questions at this level might include: What will you take from this experience and how will you relate it to your life outside of this group experience? What is something you want to remember and perhaps apply from this experience?

Good processing questions follow a "what," "so what," and "now what" format. It is important to remember that some groups will require more time at one particular level, but that none of the levels should be skipped. Allowing group members to discuss their experiences at these levels can assist them in interpreting and applying their experience at the "so what" and "now what" levels (Whichard and Kees 2006).

It is important to think through ahead of time possible processing questions at all three levels when planning your experiential activities, and then be willing to change up or add to these questions in the moment as appropriate and meaningful to your group.

Tip 74. Be conscious of your tone

In their book *Primal Leadership: Learning to Lead with Emotional Intelligence,* Goleman, Boyatzis, and McKee (2002) identify four domains of emotional intelligence: 1) self-awareness, 2) self-management, 3) social awareness, and 4) relational management. One way to show your ability to instruct from an emotionally intelligent center is to be conscious of the *tone* you use to address a group. By having emotional self-control you are better able to monitor your own internal stress levels and adjust your posture, speech tone, and volume accordingly. This form of self-control can have a big impact on the learning environment that you have worked to establish (Knowles, Holton, and Swanson 2011).

Consider video recording or audio recording your class. A few weeks later, when you have a few quiet moments, close your eyes and listen to the recording. Draw a line along a piece of paper and record an increase in your tone with a spike upward and a decrease with a spike downward. Now go back and see what you were doing at that time to elicit a change in tone. If a change in tone is matched by a need to emphasize a point or check for understanding, then great. However, you might also discover that your change in tone is excessive.

Be conscious of the tone you or someone else used for a particular session. What did the tone convey? What could have been conveyed? How? List various ways in which you could use a change in tone in your presentations or interactions.

Tip 75. Use metaphors

Framing an activity with a metaphor can help people mentally prepare for the tasks ahead and carry forward lessons learned previously. In the *Conscious Use of Metaphor in Outward Bound*, Stephen Bacon (1983) describes how the use of a figure of speech in the context of experiential learning can liken one thing to another so that new meanings become possible. Coaches, for example, are fond of saying "no pain, no gain" as they push athletes through rigorous training sessions. If taken to heart, then, the sweat and suffering can become more tolerable and understood as a necessary means to a desired end of better performances or winning games.

In designing the metaphor, consider where the group is now developmentally and where the group is going. For example, consider where they are with respect to group formation and the quality of their communication with each other or how they are functioning as a team. (See Bruce Tuckman's 1965 article on group dynamics in "forming, norming, storming, and performing.") How can you and they improve communication, teamwork, and trust?

The metaphor could be a story that helps people connect concepts. It could take the form of a saying or mantra, and be even better if it is co-created. These metaphors may be continued over many activities or sessions, and might serve as the overall theme for the program or experience. If you want more on this, Priest and Gass (2005) describe six generations of adventure facilitation that provide a great explanation of the different types of framing that are possible for an activity.

The next time you plan an experiential session, consider what metaphor(s) could enhance or deepen the impact. Make a list for the various groups you lead or know.

DEVELOP AND USE EMOTIONAL INTELLIGENCE

Dan Goleman (2009 and Howard Gardner (1983; 1999; 2000) have made strong cases for greater attention to the skills and abilities we need to navigate our own feelings, as well as what we experience with others, our "intra-personal intelligence" and our "inter-personal intelligence." Because of the challenges and potential risks involved, experiential learning puts a premium on factors like processing, communication, emotional honesty, trust, and respect.

Tip 76. Engage with tension

Emotions are an essential piece of the experiential puzzle. In *Teaching Diversity,* Ray Yang (Timpson et al. 2003) makes a strong case for the use of the Socratic approach to engage students with tension. "Should an instructor pursue an issue for pedagogical reasons even if it makes the student who broached it uncomfortable? Socratic pedagogy answers 'yes'" (82). Since the time of the ancient Greeks, many have argued that engagement is essential for learning, and especially for a deeper learning where ideas can be challenged, beliefs can be reevaluated, and new insights can emerge.

Assess your own experiences with tension, engagement, and learning. How can you increase your use of tension through Socratic interrogation? Identify those tensions that could help to energize a group and deepen the learning.

Tip 77. Challenge by choice

Karl Rohnke (1989) defines challenge as a double-edged sword. We want the lessons and activities that we present to challenge our students, but if we push too hard or too quickly, fear can shut down the learning experience. This challenge can come in various forms—physical, emotional, and/or mental. When people come to learn, they come with a self-world view (Bohm 1980), their notion of themselves and the whole world in which they live, that has been formed by a variety of factors, including their interactions with family, friends, school, and work. We often think of people leaving their comfort zones when engaging in a risky activity (bungee jumping, rock climbing, bicycle racing), but often the greatest challenges are not physical, but mental and emotional. When we challenge people to reflect critically on their self-world views, we can push them out of their emotional comfort zones. We do want to provide opportunities for people to do so in order to experience new learning, but not so abruptly that they shut down completely. Challenge by choice is a tool by which learners can control the level of risk that they are willing to take. They get to engage in the activity with the security that they can back off when they feel that there is too much pressure and they can re-engage the activity when they feel ready.

When engaging students in a new activity, take a moment to discuss the concept of "challenge by choice." Come to an agreement on group norms: how will everyone support the level of risk that any particular group member is willing to take?

Make and share a list of examples of those who valued the support they got from others to go only as far as they did, or who appreciated the push and assistance they got to go beyond what they thought they could do.

Tip 78. Get past the fear

In schools, we see many teachers who fear poor student test results or complaints from parents, and seem afraid to criticize administrative decisions. We also see many of our best students afraid to take tough classes so that they can maintain a high grade point average. We see them fearful of taking the risks that are essential for learning, worrying most about what will be on the exam. In his book on human motivation, David McClelland (1987) compares this restrictive and overly cautious "motivation to avoid failure" with a healthier "motivation to succeed" that accepts reasonable risks in the pursuit of learning.

At the heart of the second level of Shambhala training, *The Sacred Path of the Warrior,* is the Buddhist challenge to fear, that we can take responsibility for understanding and controlling our own emotional reactions. We can learn to notice our emotions without being captured, victimized, or paralyzed by them. We can "touch" those feelings, but remain centered by returning to our practiced attention on our breath. We can learn to stay open, relaxed, and present both to the reality of what we face and to our own reactions. Too often we either fold ourselves into a defensive cocoon or attack back in anger. Alternatively, Buddhists will see fear as a gift, places where we need to develop more awareness and open up.

In her now classic statement on fear, *When Things Fall Apart,* Pema Chödrön (1996, 4-5) writes: "Sometimes, however, we are cornered; everything falls apart, and we run out of options for escape…. That is where the courage comes in…. The trick is to keep exploring and not bail out, even when we find out that something is not what we thought. That's what we're going to discover again and again and again."

In her 2001 follow-up, *The Places that Scare You,* she writes:

That nothing is static or fixed, that all is fleeting and imperma-
nent, is the mark of existence. It is the ordinary state of affairs.
Everything is in process. Everything—every tree, every blade
of grass, all the animals, insects, human beings, buildings, the
animate and the inanimate—is always changing, moment to
moment. We don't have to be mystics or physicists to know
this. Yet at the level of personal experience, we resist this basic
fact. It means that life isn't always going to go our way. It means
there's loss as well as gain. And we don't like that. (2001, 23)

In *Practicing Peace in Times of War,* Chödrön (2006, 29) connects our responses to fear to bigger issues of war and peace. "Whenever there's a sense of threat, we harden. And so if we don't harden, what happens? We're left with that uneasiness, that feeling of threat. That's when the real journey of courage begins. This is the real work of the peacemaker, to find the soft spot and the tenderness in that very uneasy place and stay with it. If we can stay with the soft spot and stay with the tender heart, then we are cultivating the seeds of peace."

List your fears about teaching and learning and how experiential learning might help you move toward a "motivation to succeed."

Tip 79. Be aware of suffering

Every instructor at every level and in every discipline has some experience with what Parker Palmer termed the "student from hell," that person who is so annoying and frustrating that there is only grudging willingness to see the value of what was learned and what growth occurred. Once we understand the value of this challenge to ourselves, we have the opportunity to explore new possibilities. Noted Vietnamese monk Thich Nhat Hanh writes:

> It is only when we enter into contact with suffering that understanding and compassion can be born. Without suffering, we do not have the opportunity to cultivate compassion and understanding; and without understanding, there can be no true love....We have spoken of the organic nature of things. Suffering is also organic. It is from garbage that we produce flowers; and similarly, it is from suffering that we produce understanding and compassion. I would not want to live in a place where there is no suffering, because in such a place I would not be able to cultivate understanding and compassion, which are the basis of my happiness. Happiness is a function of compassion. If you do not have compassion in your heart, you do not have any happiness. (1998, 10-11)

Examine old experiences for the learning and insight that can come through suffering. List what you can add to an upcoming presentation or share with a group.

Tip 80. Build confidence in knowing, thinking, and acting

In *Teaching Community,* bell hooks (2003, 130) offers her insights into the problems of modern day classrooms. "In our nation, most colleges and universities are organized around the principles of dominant culture. This organizational model reinforces hierarchies of power and control. It encourages students to be fear-based, that is, to fear teachers and seek to please them. Concurrently, students are encouraged to doubt themselves, their capacities to know, to think, and to act. Learned helplessness is necessary for the maintenance of dominator culture."

List ways in which experiential learning could encourage confidence in know-ing, thinking, and acting. Offer examples from your own life. Plan a presentation that helps to build confidence in knowing, thinking, and acting.

Tip 81. Be elegant in your responses and become comfortable in your discomfort

Getting out of the routine of the presentations that you make to in-corporate experiential learning can raise new worries: What distractions will surface? How can control be maintained in the face of so much that is unpredictable? What about all those potential liability issues out of doors? What if...? What about...? In the Shambhala tradition of Bud-dhism, *elegance* has a very special and important meaning. According to Chögyam Trungpa, "Elegance means appreciating things as they are. There is a sense of delight and of fearlessness. You are not fearful of dark corners. If there are any dark or mysterious corners, black and confus-ing, you override them" (Gimian 2008, 80).

In *Leadership and the New Science*, Meg Wheatley (2001) makes a case for disequilibrium in groups and organizations, a state Piaget (1952; 1970) and others have described as essential for an individual's growth and development. "The things we fear most in organizations—disrup-tions, confusion, chaos—need not be interpreted as signs that they are about to be destroyed. Instead, these conditions are necessary to awaken creativity" (21).

Reevaluate an experience you have had that seemed disorienting at the time, even disturbing. In hindsight, what insights emerged for you? How important was that "disequilibrium"? List the ways in which you can become more comfortable with the kinds of discomfort that can lead to developmental shifts for individuals and groups. When you consider some experiential activity, try reframing any wor-ries you have within the context of the "elegance" with which you could face any-thing new and different, as challenges that can delight and engage you, and fears that you can override.

Tip 82. Embrace change

Change can be very challenging, both emotionally and intellectu-ally. Scholars like Howard Gardner (1983; 1999; 2000) and Dan Goleman (2009) want us to pay greater attention to the emotional requirements in experiential learning for both "intrapersonal" and "interpersonal" intelligence. Feelings arise and often require attention and skill to navigate. The good news is that these "skills" are learnable and teachable. In *Primal Leadership*, Goleman, Boyatzis, and McKee (2002) make the case for emotional intelligence in leadership. "Whatever a leader's repertoire of styles today, it can grow wider tomorrow. The key lies in strengthening the underlying emotional intelligence abilities that drive a given style. Leadership is learnable.... The process is not easy. It takes time and, most of all, commitment. But the benefits that flow from leadership with a well-developed emotional intelligence, both for the individual and the organization, make it not only worthwhile but invigorating" (88).

Identify experiences when you embraced change, when you feared it. In your experience, when has leadership reflected a "well-developed emotional intelligence." List the key players and what their skills were.

Tip 83. Develop trust

Christine Aguilar and Nereida Perdigon spent time together in a graduate seminar that incorporated experiential learning in a mountain retreat setting and reflected on its content regarding educational leadership, renewal, and change. They expressed the following: "We know that there are some 1,400 students and scholars from 85 countries at our university who are engaged in academic work and research both on and off campus. We also know that these people could, under the right circumstances, contribute more to the creative synergy that is possible with this degree of diversity. When planning experiential learning, however, we must consider how those beliefs might impact someone's ability to participate or learn in ways that instructors may not have envisioned." In Michael Fullan's (2005) *Leadership and Sustainability*, Aguilar and Perdigon found this statement relevant: "High-trust cultures make the extraordinary possible, energizing people and giving them the wherewithal to be successful under enormously demanding conditions and the confidence that staying the course will pay off" (2005, 73).

Identify those times and places when you felt that your organizational culture made the "extraordinary possible," energizing you and others even under "enormously demanding conditions." What could you do to build more of a "high-trust culture" in your organization?

TEACH HOLISTICALLY

When we focus too intently on content without much concern for those who are attending, we violate basic principles of effective instruction. By knowing more about our audiences, we can pay attention to their motivation. We can also try to make the material meaningful and relevant to their lives and interests. Experiential learning can tap into all the senses, providing us useful information about a group, as well as offering them different paths into the topic or concept under study.

Tip 84. Find the courage to teach

With the publication of *The Courage to Teach* in 1998, Parker Palmer tapped into a very big and receptive audience with his challenge to teachers everywhere to be genuine, to connect the head and heart, the brain and the emotions, for themselves and their students. He opens with this statement: "I am a teacher at heart, and there are moments in the classroom when I can hardly hold the joy. When my students and I discover uncharted territory to explore, when the pathways out of the thicket open up before us, when our experience is illuminated by the lightning-life of the mind—then teaching is the finest work I know. But at other moments, the classroom is so lifeless or painful or confused—and I am so powerless to do anything about it—that my claim to be a teacher seems a transparent sham" (1998, 1).

List those moments when experience allowed you to connect head and heart, energizing your teaching or learning and allowing you to discover new insights.

Tip 85. Be aware of complexity and ambiguity

According to Perry (1981; 1999), we move beyond dichotomous, right-wrong, yes-no thinking as we mature intellectually; we learn to hear and understand other perspectives, and how to handle complexity and ambiguity. In his seminal model of moral development, Lawrence Kohlberg (1963) sees humans moving beyond strict obedience to develop ethical principles that can guide their thinking. The Buddhist leader Chögyam Trungpa once wrote, "When we talk of emptiness, it means the absence of solidity, the absence of fixed notions which cannot be changed" (Gimian 2008, 69). In our research on learning, we have come to see how the higher levels of cognitive and moral development reflect a similar openness to other views, to ideas that are different or new. Experiential learning can offer those different and new perspectives.

Review a recent troubling experience and concentrate on avoiding any oversimplification of the issues. Practice embracing the richness of the inherent complexities and ambiguities to see where these could lead.

DEEPEN LEARNING

Paul Ramsden (1992) notes the difference between *surface* learning and its emphasis on knowledge that is often delivered through lecture and assessed through objective means (multiple choice or true-false exam items) and *deep* learning that can emerge through experiential learning and assessed through observation, written papers, projects, and presentations.

Tip 86. Reduce the amount to be covered and go for deeper learning

In the opening pages of *Tools for Teaching*, Barbara Davis makes a plea for covering less and focusing instead on student learning. "In developing or revising a course, faculty are faced with at least three critical decisions: what to teach, how to teach it, and how to ensure that students are learning what is being taught. Often the most difficult step in preparing or revising a course is deciding what topics must be excluded if the topic is to be manageable. Many teachers, hoping to impart to students everything they know about a subject, attempt to include too much material by a half" (1993, 3).

Paul Ramsden has written about surface and deep learning, how a preoccupation with note taking, memorization, and multiple choice exams emphasizes our "acquired knowledge," but rarely does much to develop our abilities to apply that learning, or to know how to evaluate and integrate different sources. A recurrent finding of this research into student learning is that we can never assume that the impact of teaching on learning is what we expect it to be:

Students' thoughts and actions are profoundly affected by the educational context or environment in which they learn. They react to the demands of teaching and assessment in ways that are difficult to predict: A lot of their 'learning' is not directly about chemistry or history or economics, but about learning how to please lecturers and gain high marks. These strategies all too often lead them into using methods of study that focus on simply recalling and reproducing information rather than the actions which will lead to change in their understanding. (1992, 89-90)

In *Turning the Mind into an Ally*, Sakyong Mipham (2003, 188) writes about the power of meditation to help us go deeper. "If we're meditating properly, our practice and understanding will always take us a little further than we might think we want to go. By resting in the true meaning of our contemplation, we're becoming familiar with our wisdom. We're beginning to see reality as it is. Just as we open our perspective beyond what we ever thought it could be, our wisdom thrusts us into yet a vaster world. This is how we keep moving on the path. At each stage of contemplative meditation, we're encouraging a deeper level of knowing."

When planning to incorporate experiential learning, begin with a reevaluation of the amount of content you want to cover and what you could eliminate or address in other ways. List your goals in some kind of rank order so that you will have adequate time to process the experiences before moving on to new content. Use meditation, journaling, or reflective time to step back from an experience and tap into a deeper understanding of core concepts that lie below the surface. List those insights and their meaning for an upcoming presentation or activity.

Tip 87. Use long term projects to help tie together learning, experience, and development

When you can work with people on a longer term basis (for more than a single class or workshop), you have several advantages. One of these is that you are able to develop long-term projects which can create a deeper, broader picture of everyone's abilities. Consider the creation of an academic portfolio. Over time this can become more than a collection of papers and coursework. Rather, as Brandes and Boskic note, an academic portfolio can create an environment where knowledge is shared and constructed. It can also help individuals focus on "reflection and deepening (their) understanding of learning" (2008, 1). Brandes and

Boskic also found that over time and with more experience, portfolios became more than chronological organizations of information. Rather, they illustrated cognitive and developmental processes, serving as catalysts that enhanced intellectual organization.

List several projects that would encourage a deeper picture of development.

Tip 88. See basic goodness in very simple experiences

Along with new insights and the potential for new growth, opening up to new experiences can offer even deeper lessons about the very nature of life and our selves. Chögyam Trungpa, the Buddhist teacher who brought the teachings of the Shambhala lineage to the US and founded Naropa University, offers this perspective.

> Discovering real goodness comes from appreciating very simple experiences....We experience glimpses of goodness all the time, but we often fail to acknowledge them. When we see a bright color, we are witnessing our own inherent goodness. When we hear a beautiful sound, we are hearing our own basic goodness. When we step out of the shower, we feel fresh and clean, and when we walk out of a stuffy room, we appreciate the sudden whiff of fresh air. These events may take a fraction of a second, but they are real experiences of goodness. (1984, 12)

List those moments of joy you have had through direct experience, no matter how simple, and how you were reminded of this "basic goodness of life."

ENCOURAGE DISCOVERY AND CREATIVITY

There is much research on the nature of discovery and how people can deepen their understanding through hands on activities. There are also many links between discovery and creativity, how a willingness to explore and undertake new experiences can broaden our thinking. With discovery and creativity, as with experiential learning, we get to explore and reflect, analyze, and evaluate in ways that aren't prescribed.

Tip 89. Focus on metacognition

Experiential learning draws on many aspects of effective instruction including metacognition for, at its core, we are asking people to step back from some activity and make sense of their reactions, thoughts, and feelings. The focus shifts away from acquired or memorized knowledge. In *Metateaching and the Instructional Map,* Bill Timpson describes the basics of inquiry or discovery learning. "One of the more challenging approaches to teaching, discovery learning or inquiry, attempts to foster critical and creative thinking, to help students better understand their own thinking processes (metacognition), and to give students experiences with problem solving in which answers may be complex and in which different perspectives and approaches are possible" (1999, 94).

Reflect on what you have been able to discover from your more memorable learning experiences. List the ways in which you can emphasize discovery in an upcoming program or presentation.

Tip 90. Cultivate intelligence while accepting "ignorance"

When thinking about the learning process and how much students need to discover on their own, Lowell Wightman, an experienced teacher and coach at many levels, was taken by the arguments of Michael Fullan (2005, 8) about the change process. "First there is the myth that ignorance is a solvable problem. Ignorance is not a solvable problem; it is rather an inescapable part of the human condition." Wightman caught himself trying to solve the problem of "ignorance" among his students, becoming frustrated and disappointed when he failed. "Fullan reminds me that my students have thresholds and limits to their intellectual capacity that I should understand." As teachers, experience allows us to step back from our frustrations and see students in an honest, accurate light. Experience can also allow students to see their own limitations in different contexts.

Reflect on the struggles that you have had teaching others. Identify those times when their "ignorance" proved more difficult to overcome than you had initially expected. As you work with discovery, make a note to yourself about accepting this "inescapable part of the human condition." List those additional experiences that would broaden and deepen your assessment of student talent.

Tip 91. Rekindle a childlike imagination

Recalling his early years on the reservation, Goldlin Wall remembers that "our imaginations could run wild and we could see ourselves doing the impossible and the incredible." Egan describes the potential for this kind of "classroom as a place from which one takes off into other environments, so that [teachers] can easily engage students' imaginations in learning" (2005, 248). Yet, once formal schooling began, Goldlin found that his education was all too often dominated by a teaching style based on lecturing and textbooks, memorization and routine.

Can you recall a time where you had to use your imagination in a college class? List ways in which you could recapture the excitement and enthusiasm you had as a child by providing real life experiences and tying these into the classroom.

Tip 92. Look to business for innovation

In *The Courage to Teach,* Parker Palmer notes: "Most major corporations have in-house 'universities' to help their employees keep pace with rapid change in society, technology, and markets. For example, each of the Big Six accountancy firms 'operates its own education division to provide continuing, graduate-level education to its professional employees. It is not uncommon for a firm to manage over a million contact hours of training each year.' Nor is it uncommon for these nontraditional programs to employ pedagogies more inventive that one can find at most colleges and schools" (1998, 178).

If you had control over a substantial professional development program, what experiences would you emphasize? How would you encourage inventiveness?

Tip 93. Explore case-based, problem-based, and project-based learning

Barrows and Tamblyn (1980) note how professional roles typically defy overly reductionistic reasoning. With case-based learning, an approach that is especially popular in law and business schools, the instructor's role is to guide students through an exploration of the central issues in a particular case, explaining how to access various sources and what the possible interpretations could be. The same arguments could be made for problem-based learning, which is widely used in medical schools, and project-based learning, which often serves as a concluding experience for engineering programs. In essence, learning becomes an immersion in an issue and a process for exploration. Based on their work at the Harvard Business School, where the case study method has been practiced and refined over many years, Barnes, Christensen, and Hansen (1994) have laid out compelling reasons for this approach to instruction and learning. As tangible expressions of Bloom's (1956) "Taxonomy" in the cognitive domain, these cases, problems, and projects offer students opportunities to *apply* their *knowledge* within a context of real world examples, and to deepen their *understanding* through *analysis, synthesis,* and *evaluation.*

Identify cases, problems, or projects that could engage your students or audiences in an exploration of meaningful issues. Make a list of ideas for an upcoming presentation or class session.

EXPLORE ALTERNATIVE APPROACHES

You can learn much about people by seeing them in different contexts—active, interactive, exploring a new environment or responding to a different kind of challenge, as part of a team or working independently. You also can learn much about your own teaching or group facilitation, stretching to make good use of new environments or activities and responding to the reactions of others. As you expect others to explore and reflect, analyze, and evaluate, so will you.

Tip 94. Do not clone yourself

Feeling alienated from colleagues can undermine motivation and productivity. For example, the research of Sheila Tobias (1990) documents the loss of talented students from classes where the style of teaching does not match their own preferences. Specifically, Tobias noted how talented students were leaving science majors that required heavy memorization and where they were graded on a competitive curve. Instead they were opting for disciplines where they could see their future in more cooperative, supportive environments. She explained this migration of talent as a reaction to a "cloning process" where predominantly older white males taught in ways that mirrored how they were taught. Not only were many talented students discouraged by this style, a disproportionate number were females and minority students, further compounding the problem for these science disciplines.

Identify past experiences when you were discouraged by a traditional delivery style that was overly competitive and isolating. Commit to exploring new uses of experiential learning to augment formal presentations. Use these to generate insights into the range of learning styles and preferences that could be tapped. List what you could try differently in an upcoming presentation.

Tip 95. Use wait time

In the classroom, wait time is a concept that has proven important in the research literature on learning yet it is problematic for many teachers. Too often, teachers limit the time students need to reflect, especially when they have been through an engaging, moving experience. Silence seems so difficult. We come to the aid of students who are unsure or hesitant whereas some "space" (time, encouragement) may be exactly what is needed to see another solution or find the right words. Moreover, some students need that extra amount of time to be able to formulate their responses. These are the people who often defer to more extroverted members of the group, but by so doing rob themselves of the benefits of working ideas out on their own. Too often they sit back and let others do the work. Some people also seem more likely to work out their thinking in public settings. They are by nature talkative and often gain insight into their own thinking through interaction with others. Put them in a quiet space to think it all through and they struggle. Others, however, are by nature more reflective and cautious. They want to ponder and sleep on issues.

Drawing on research by Rowe (1974), Jeanne Ormrod describes it his way:

> When teachers ask students a question, they typically wait one second or less for a response. If students don't respond in that short time interval, teachers tend to speak again—sometimes by asking different students the same question, sometimes by rephrasing the question, sometimes even by answering the question themselves.... Teachers are equally reluctant to let much time elapse after students answer questions or make comments in class. (1998, 259)

Referring to Giaconia's (1987) research, Gage and Berliner add this additional note: "If you ask a higher level question, you need to give students more time to think about the answer. Students need time to process information. Yet ... teachers did not tend to wait longer after they asked higher-order questions" (1998, 485). In other words, to get more thoughtful responses, asking open-ended or divergent questions or asking students to analyze, synthesize, or evaluate, will typically require some time and space, perhaps through writing or small group discussions. For teachers, this also means a shift from direct instruction to the facilitation of learning.

In their collection of tips for teaching sustainability, Timpson et al. recommend that teachers shift from statements to questions and then factor in the wait time needed for students to adequately process complex and challenging issues: "Learning how to question—to challenge conventional wisdom and rethink the prevailing paradigm—has been a hallmark of learning dating back to the earliest writings of the Greek philosophers" (2006, 147).

Writing about diversity, a complex and sensitive subject, Timpson et al. ask teachers to pause and reflect on a regular basis: "Students are often overwhelmed with the amount of information that comes at them in class. Discussions can also be problematic when opinions range widely and students are unsure what to focus on and put into their notes. Find ways of pausing in class for you and your students to reflect. Use a brief free-write, or try counting silently to yourself to provide a little more 'wait time' to help students come up with thoughtful responses to complex questions. Pause and review periodically to help underscore key points and reinforce conceptual framework that helps to keep everything connected" (2005, 20).

Finally, it is important for teachers to know that wait time also supports what researchers refer to as the necessary incubation period that underlies creative thinking. Patrick (1955), for example, insists that teachers have to let ideas simmer and then pay attention to what emerges. This can take considerable time and engender some real frustrations as students break through conventional thinking about the "right" answers.

Practice counting to yourself for five seconds after you have asked a group a question and before you entertain a response. Note what changes.

Tip 96. Analyze the hidden price tag

Known for his work on *emotional intelligence,* Daniel Goleman also put forward arguments for *ecological intelligence,* the awareness of the environmental impact of our actions, choices, and values—the "capacity to recognize the hidden web of connections between human activity and nature's systems and the subtle complexities of their interactions" (2009, 43). For example, one way to do this is to analyze the hidden environmental costs of various products that we may be using for experiential learning.

> Our world of material abundance comes with a hidden price tag. We cannot see the extent to which the things we buy and use daily have other kinds of costs—their toll on the planet, on consumer health, and on the people whose labor provides us our comforts and necessities. We go through our daily life awash in a sea of things we buy, use, and throw away, waste, or save. Each of these things has its own history and its own future, back stories and endings largely hidden from our eyes, a web of impacts left along the way from the initial extraction or concoction of its ingredients, during its manufacture and transport, through the subtle consequences of its use in our homes and workplaces, to the day we dispose of it. And yet these unseen impacts of all that stuff may be their most important aspect. (2009, 2)

Evaluate the full history of the various products that you will be using for an experiential learning exercise including paper, pens and pencils, shoes, clothes, water bottles, sunscreen, insect repellant, backpacks, cell phones, etc. Plan to have others do the same. Evaluate the "environmental or ecological footprint" needed to produce each item. You can also analyze issues of fair labor costs and safe working conditions. Whatever materials you use can be an opportunity to incorporate experiential learning as you explore their origins.

Tip 97. Energize and re-engage participants

In *Concepts and Choices for Teaching,* Timpson and Doe make a basic case for experiential learning.

> We can enlarge our teaching repertoire to include many alternatives to the traditional lecture and, having learned from our experiences with these alternatives, we can discover and improve the approaches that work best for us…While these approaches can require an investment of time to fully experience and process, they can be stimulating and fun, providing some

very welcomed variety.... Getting a class energized with some kind of active, experiential learning can help re-engage students. While there is no substitute for careful planning, some instructors will also grab an opportunity that presents itself in class to try something different, for example, to stage a mini-debate on an issue that arises in discussion, ask *"What if?"* questions and explore student thinking with a spontaneous simulation, or have students try out their ideas in role-plays. (2008, 273-274)

Identify those experiences in your life that helped to energize and re-engage your learning. List your reasons for wanting to utilize more experiential learning.

Tip 98. Practice for mastery and walk your talk

In *Primal Leadership: Learning to Lead with Emotional Intelligence,* Dan Goleman and his team make a compelling case for the importance of practice in developing and mastering new skills. Too often, instructors focus all their energy on coverage, somehow believing that explaining a certain concept and even demonstrating a new skill is enough to ensure learning.

Great athletes spend a lot of time practicing and a little time performing, while executives spend no time practicing and all of their time performing.... No wonder leaders so often recycle their problems: In the rush to achieve their goals and complete their tasks, they short themselves on learning to lead better. Often, a leader will try a new approach once or twice, and then apply it—without giving himself the chance to *practice* it. The key to learning new habits for leaders lies in practice to the point of mastery. (2002, 157)

Val Middleton was bothered by the resistance she often faced when teaching about diversity to her classes of future teachers. Instead of blaming the students, she decided to explore her own experience of resistance. "In an effort to 'walk my talk,' I wanted the experience of silently listening to someone else share values and beliefs that could likely be in opposition to mine. After thoughtful, but fretful, consideration, I decided to go to church after years of avoidance. Growing up in the Pentecostal tradition, I was told to listen to the voice of God or there literally would be 'hell to pay'" (Middleton 2003, 105).

Remind yourself of when you were able to take the time to really practice a new skill and deepen your understanding before you had to put it into play. Remind yourself about those times when you had to rush something into play. Identify what was different. Rethink an upcoming project to ensure the practice time you want and need. List what you would do differently. Make a list of those places and activities that would challenge you to be true to your values and better understand the reactions of others. Use a journal to reflect on your reactions and insights.

Tip 99. Model what you want

In their classic text for instructors in higher education, Marilla Svinicki and Bill McKeachie (2011) make a strong case for the importance of modeling, how an instructor's actions augment the content and deepen the learners' experiences. What teachers do impacts what others learn. "A teacher, whether by accident or by design, is more to students than a content expert. The teacher is a model of all that it means to be a scholar, a thinking person. We teach not only what we know but also what we are. Part of the ethics of teaching is to realize this responsibility and to become the best models we can be, which requires serious self-reflection on our personal standards of scholarship and learning" (321).

Rethink an upcoming presentation and list what you could do to model what you want learned. The experience will also teach you much.

Tip 100. Be authentic

Jacqueline McGinty writes about her experiences teaching adult education classes. "I have found that when I become too entrenched in my use of a particular teaching method, I become less authentic. In contrast, when I come to class full of excitement for the material and the students, and I'm eager to share, I rarely think about methods. I like to provide variety in my classes, but when I become too concerned over my teaching methods I lose touch with the present moment. In *The Courage to Teach,* Parker Palmer (1998, 6) described it this way: 'Technique is what teachers use until the real teacher arrives.'"

Identify those moments when you have felt both authentic and effective as an instructor. List ways in which you could increase both in the future.

Tip 101. Commit to self-care, relationships, growth, values, and balance

Skovholt (2001) suggests that there is much to be learned from teachers about their needs for staying healthy, active, and professional. More than seventy practitioners at different stages of their careers took part in this formal qualitative research project designed to identify the "teacher's voice." The themes that emerged include the following: First, nearly every respondent mentioned some variation on the themes of carving out time for physical exercise and taking care to eat well. Second, personal connections provided a social buffer against the stressors inherent in the job. Third, setting annual personal and professional development goals along with dedicating time for intellectual renewal were important for avoiding stagnation and burnout. Fourth, principles and values were the guiding forces in deciding what was worthwhile. Fifth, balancing personal and professional worlds became essential.

Use these five principles to evaluate your experiences as a teacher or presenter. List areas where you could improve.

Tip 102. Research, write, and produce a magazine, newsletter, or other publication

Motivation has always been a hot topic in educational circles. What can we do to pique student interest and how can we teach content with that in mind? In the 1970s and 1980s, Robert Gardner and Wallace Lambert demonstrated that with a positive attitude comes the motivation to learn (Gardner 1985). More recently, Dörnyei (2001) identified key criteria that stimulate motivation: the task, the autonomy, the creativity, and the corrective feedback. According to Grim (2010), giving authentic opportunities to students can also have an impact on motivation. If you combine all the key ingredients in a magazine project, you get motivation to learn content as well as cooperation, risk taking, and organizational skills.

When designing or rethinking a course or wanting to engage an organization at a deeper level, consider researching, writing, and producing your own publication to which students and colleagues could contribute. The experience could prove invaluable for everyone.

Tip 103. Rethink hegemonic assumptions

We are often trapped in unnoticed or controlling assumptions in our daily interactions. A hegemonic assumption is one that we accept as natural or real without critically analyzing underlying assumptions (Brookfield 2005). We come to accept them, yet we may have never explored how we came to integrate them into our social construct of reality. For example, you could pick a topic that is well understood and accepted by most people in a specific culture, the value of schooling for instance. But then ask yourself: Where does this belief originate? How is it propagated? What forms of social control does this belief reinforce? Is it possible that certain people are oppressed by this belief? What role does the media play? By opening a discussion that explores a concept like this you can generate critical reflection and analysis on important questions, for example, when do experiences become more important than classroom or book learning?

Take a relatively common social belief and critically analyze how this belief became accepted and how it is propagated in your culture or community. How can experience change that belief?

TAP INTO THE CREATIVE ARTS

There is always much we learn through the creative arts—how, for example, writers and filmmakers can draw characters and describe events that capture the richness that is experiential learning. In what follows, you will see what can be mined from stories, both fictional and documentary. Know that engagement, so essential in theater and film, is at the heart of effective experiential learning.

Tip 104. Find examples in literature, television, film, and theater

In an inspiring autobiographical account, a young African boy, William Kamkwamba (2009) describes his life on small farm in Malawi, the hard work needed to put food on the table for himself, his parents, and sisters, and the brutal realities of drought and poor government planning that put the costs for needed fertilizers out of reach or that squandered the nation's agricultural reserves, spiraling the lives of poor farmers, in particular, down as the ravages of famine emaciated the population. Corruption, greed, and ignorance kept simple farmers and their village neighbors on the edge of survival year after year, no matter how hard everyone worked or how simply they lived. Yet, despite these hardships, Kamkwamba showed a deep desire to learn, to get an education that would lift him out of this tough and unpredictable existence. For poor families, school fees always remained an obstacle, and William was like so many others who could not pay to go on.

However, unlike so many of his peers who sunk into a life of deferred hopes and dreams, hard labor, or the pleasures of the drinking life, Kamkwamba found a library at the nearby elementary school where Americans had donated books on a range of subjects. Without the demands of formal schooling, and needing to keep his mind engaged, he began to explore what resources could help his family withstand the next downward shock. In particular, he wanted to know more about the electricity that was generated down river by the hydroelectric plant and if the river nearby could produce something similar for his family. Could that power be harnessed to pump water form deeper wells and produce another crop, that something extra that could protect his family from the next shock and the ever present threat of starvation?

Despite very limited English, and with the help of the librarian, he began to work his way through whatever reading material he could find, even texts on physics, studying the diagrams and deciphering the related descriptions as best he could. The scrap yard nearby became his laboratory as he began to explore this world of mechanics, finally fixing on the ever steady supply of wind that might drive small generators and produce the electricity that his family could otherwise not afford. Endless cycles of trial and error and further study allowed Kamkwamba to experiment with the ways that local spare parts and makeshift substitutes could begin to approximate the wind turbines he had read about or seen in diagrams.

Identify examples of experiential learning in the stories you have found to be important and meaningful. List several ways in which you could incorporate more of these kinds of stories in an upcoming presentation?

Tip 105. Add drama to your lessons and use inspiring stories

In *Teaching and Performing: Ideas for Energizing your Classes,* Bill Timpson and Suzanne Burgoyne critique traditional instruction that attempts only to impart information. "Good teaching is more than giving information. In this day of desk-top publishing and Internet resources, class notes are easily updated, reproduced, and made available to students to copy, put on reserve at the library, or included on a course web site. Why not use class time for interactions, debates, discussions, questions, role plays, activities, and opportunities to practice new skills—all meaningful ways to develop students' talents? Few members of the general public would attend performances during which scripts are merely read. They want more, and so do students. Great teachers use many of the skills of great performers to bring their lecture notes—their 'scripts' —to life" (2002, 44-45).

In his riveting book of survival and innovation, Kamkwamba goes on to describe how his simple, home-made windmill proved successful and attracted the attention of government officials, the media, and some investors. Eventually, he got the opportunity to travel to the US and see a wind farm in Palm Springs, California. He writes:

> As I watched them, they seemed to be telling me some-thing—that I didn't have to decide just then. I could return to Africa and go back to school, reclaim the life that had been taken from me for so long. And after that, who knows? Perhaps I would study these machines and learn how to build them, then plant my own forest of them along the green fields of Ma-lawi. Perhaps I would teach others to build more simple wind-mills like the one I had at home, to provide their own light and water without having to depend on the government. Perhaps I'd do both. But whatever it was I decided to do, I would apply this lesson I'd learned: If you want to make it, all you have to do is try (2009, 281).

Reflect on a past lesson or lecture and imagine how it could have been ener-gized and the learning deepened. List ideas for adding experiential elements to an upcoming presentation. Think about those times when you were able to learn from trial and error or help others be resourceful and solve the problems that they faced. Describe how future lessons could be reframed to encourage this kind of experiential learning.

Tip 106. Teach others to make a difference and celebrate the magic

Drawing on a successful experience can help inspire others to do something similar and create an even bigger benefit. Later in his book, Kamkwamba describes how he inspired an audience in his native Ma-lawi. "I walked them through the steps of how I'd built everything using simple scrapyard materials, and I hoped I'd inspire them to build some-thing themselves. *If I can teach my neighbors how to build windmills,* I thought, *what else can we build together?* 'In science we invent and create,' I said. 'We make new things that can benefit our situation. If we can all invent something and put it to work, we can change Malawi" (2009, 249).

It can take real courage to defy the norm and strike out in new directions. Galileo had to defy the "facts" of the day that put the earth at the center of the universe. He challenged what he was taught by teachers and risked an indictment of heresy from priests because the data, the positions of the stars, suggested a different explanation. For anyone who is willing to explore new interpretations, there is always the risk of censure, ridicule, or worse.

When the famine hit Malawi and the reasons why proved unclear, the boy experimenter, Kamkwamba, was an easy target. "During the summer of 2002, the people of our area blamed the unpopular Muluzi government, venting their rage on the corrupt officials who'd sold our maize surplus. But this time, instead of acknowledging the cruel weather, they began blaming magic. And that meant blaming me... 'It's not a machine—it's a witch tower. The boy is calling witches.' 'Wait!' I screamed. 'The drought is all over the country. It's not just here. Electric wind (what Kamkwamba was generating with his home-made wind tower) is not the cause.' 'But we saw it with our own eyes!' they said. I became very afraid that these people would collect a mob and tear down my windmill or worse. I kept a low profile for the next week, stayed inside, and even stopped the blades during the day so they wouldn't raise more suspicions" (2009, 239, 243).

William Kamkwamba has made two TED talks on his wind tower and how it changed his life. See the URL's:

http://www.ted.com/talks/william_kamkwamba_on_building_a_windmill.html

http://www.ted.com/talks/william_kamkwamba_how_i_harnessed_the_wind.html

---

Make a list of those changes you have seen or know about that have been inspired by one person's experience. How can you rethink a future project? Make a list of examples or experiences you can cite that could inspire others. Identify those times when you or someone you know took criticism for straying outside the lines when exploring new ideas or possibilities. How could these memories help you rethink a future presentation or project?

MAKE USE OF STORYTELLING

The oral tradition goes back to our earliest understanding of humans and the societies that they created, the values, beliefs, and wisdom that they passed down to their children and subsequent generations. With an attention to the details of an important experience—colors, smells, sights, sounds, geography, people, and events—audiences and students will engage and remember more.

Tip 107. Tell more stories and encourage transformative learning

In *Teaching and Learning Peace,* Bill Timpson (2002) makes a case for the use of stories that draw on past experiences from the real world. "Stories can be powerfully simple mechanisms to engage audiences and stimulate learning. The rich details of lives, events, and places draw us in and speak volumes about underlying beliefs and values. Without analysis or judgment, we are left to come to our own conclusions, much like audiences in the theater" (107).

Callahan et al. (2009) describe how the use of narrative techniques, or storytelling, can help people reflect critically on a life experience. This becomes important for achieving "transformative learning" where individuals make meaning of an experience and then incorporate changes into their lives. As a facilitator, you can share your own stories of how you have experienced or lived a topic being explored in class. The sharing of self through the narrative becomes a way for people to see a personal interaction with a topic, as well as how stories and self-disclosure can help build community. For example, you might share an example of how you have been marginalized at some point in time and what you changed in your life as a way to personalize the focus on critical theory and its analysis of power and privilege.

Remembering how stories were told around the campfire, augment an experience you have had with the details of place and character, sounds and smells, plot twists and turns that will more fully engage listeners and deepen their understanding of your experience and the important lessons you learned. List experiences that you have had that might relate to a topic you want to address. How might you put those experiences into a narrative that you could share? In what ways could you encourage people to put their own experiences into story form to share and reflect upon?

PROMOTE POSITIVE VALUES AND MORAL DEVELOPMENT

Active and interactive learning often highlight the values that underlie our reactions. Despite what we say we believe, the deeper "truth" is often in our actions. Our experiences can reveal much about our own thinking. These examples can help clarify insights and deepen our understanding.

Tip 108. Use a framework for moral development and develop dilemmas

In his seminal model of moral development, Kohlberg (1963) sees humans moving up through a hierarchy. At level one, people respond out of obedience or fear. At level two, people think of reciprocity, why they would respond in a certain way because they expected similar treatment from others. At level three, people want to be considered "good." At the fourth level, people think about law and order. At level five, they think about social contracts and individual rights, and at level six, the focus is on universal ethical principles. His model can serve as a useful reference for evaluating our experiences, actions, and plans for the future.

Within his groundbreaking work on a hierarchy of moral development, Kohlberg always insisted that it would be essential for people of all ages to be actively engaged in provocative dilemmas that could then serve as catalysts for their growth and development in moral reasoning. The experience of being immersed in a complex situation can challenge people to move past lower levels of moral thinking. Although Carol Gilligan (1993) would later argue for more attention to the role of relationships in the thinking of females, it would still be the power of direct involvement in dilemmas by participants that would reveal their underlying reasoning.

Measure a past action against Kohlberg's stages of moral development. Consider what that means for the future. Identify those moral dilemmas that have pushed you to develop and clarify your own thinking about ethical issues. Include a moral dilemma in an upcoming session to challenge people to assess their thinking within the framework that Kohlberg and Gilligan provide.

Tip 109. Connect the dots

With its ability to fully engage participants and offer insights that are nearly impossible in the formal classroom setting, experiential learning can be very powerful and memorable. However, its benefits can be fleeting for students if we do not "connect the dots" and help them transfer learning to their academic studies or work. In *The Last Refuge,* noted ecologist David Orr identifies all those factors that must be seen in their web of interrelationships if we are to respond to the environmental threats we can see so clearly. "We now have to move quickly from fossil fuels to renewable energy and must establish sustainable practices in agriculture and forestry, rebuild habitable cities, construct an ecologically viable transportation system, protect biological diversity, create sustainable communities, safeguard air and water quality, eliminate toxics, and, not least, distribute wealth fairly within and between generations. These, however, are not separate or separable things, but are rather part of a larger pattern. They require us to understand the connections between how we provision ourselves with energy, food, and shelter and issues of economic prosperity, fairness, security, and democracy" (2004, 5).

"Connect the dots" with important experiential learning in your own life, that is, identify the interrelationships that exist for environmental, economic and societal well being, the most common definition of sustainability. How could you help people see these connections in an activity you could introduce in an upcoming presentation?

WORK DIRECTLY WITH DATA

Inductive thinking allows us to make sense of the experiences we have, stepping back from our reactions to group and label our insights. Feedback and assessments are essential aspects of learning that help us revise and refine our thinking. The evaluation of experiences is much more subjective and complex than traditional classroom assessment, but still valuable.

Tip 110. Have faith in direct experience

Galileo was taught that the earth was the center of the universe. He had to defy the prevailing wisdom of the day, as well as the charges of heresy from priests, to see contravening data in the stars and planets themselves. In his cataloging of different plants and animals, Darwin had to abandon all the creation stories that ruled the day and draw new insights from the similarities and differences he could see directly.

In *Concepts and Choices for Teaching,* Bill Timpson and Sue Doe (2008) describe the essence of discovery or constructivist learning as approaches where students get to explore an issue, topic or problem first through observation and hands-on experiences before wrestling with what the defining principles or underlining concepts might be. For Sakyong Mipham, there is a core Buddhist principle that is very similar at play:

> What is nonconceptual understanding? It's the intuitive insight that knows the truth directly, not through reason or logic, but beyond the realm of thought.... It's said that seeing is believ-

ing—yet nonconceptual understanding is beyond belief....This is where *prajna* takes us—beyond. True reality is beyond concept, beyond the duality of this and that. True *prajna,* true knowledge, is direct experience. It's knowing without the filter of self. Direct experience is wisdom itself—unborn, unceasing, neither still nor moving (2003, 190).

Identify examples from your own life when you had to overcome what you were taught to see the true nature of reality.

Tip 111. Rethink your thoughts

Inductive thinking can make use of the "data" from experience to raise awareness about alternative explanations. As instructors we get to revisit established ideas in a new light. As students, we get to move beyond rote memorization and construct our own interpretations. In *Teaching and Learning Peace,* Bill Timpson (2002) describes how tragic it was for native peoples in the Americas when they faced early European explorers and settlers who saw them only as "savages" to be exploited, eliminated, or converted. In many Pennsylvania colonies, in contrast, there was much less bloodshed between native peoples and white settlers because the Quakers only saw other humans and, importantly, refused to use weapons to settle their differences. Michael Carroll connects this process to a meditation practice: "When we commit to the present moment by coming back to our breath, we discover that we have not really been experiencing our world all along. Instead, we have been experiencing *our thoughts about the world.* When we leap into the present moment, we experience the world as *empty* of those thoughts: we experience our world directly rather than conceptually" (2008, 101).

Identify previous experiences when you were able to see reality in ways that were different from what you had been taught. Begin with the "data" of those experiences, that is, the sights, sounds, actions, reactions, and emotions. Consider how these data could be organized and labeled. What interpretations or hypotheses are possible? Describe how you could help others make a similar kind of shift.

Tip 112. Look and look further

In our fast-paced, goal-driven world, many people push to be efficient with their time. With music or television often in the background, they attempt to multitask as much as possible. Their cell phones keep them in constant contact with others. Students in class and people at meetings often have their laptops open, answering email or surfing the Internet. Yet, we have to ask, at what cost to their ability to concentrate, understand, and fully engage with others?

Buddhist teacher Chögyam Trungpa encourages us to resist the temptations to do more and, instead, see what we can discover when we slow down and look again. "Open your eyes, don't blink, and look—look further. Then you might *see* something. The more you look, the more inquisitive you are, the more you are bound to see....You appreciate the world around you. It is a fantastic new discovery of the world" (Gimian 2008, 78-79).

Replay a recent action and this time pause to "look again" and notice what more you can see or feel. Plan to do this in an upcoming presentation or activity.

Tip 113. Stay balanced and centered

There is always value in staying balanced and centered, aware of what is working as well as being open to possible improvements. When Bill Timpson conducts a mid-semester student feedback session in university classes, he always begins with a cataloging of what students appreciate before turning to concerns and recommendations for improvements (Timpson and Doe 2008). It's too easy to fall into blaming, complaining, indicting, and worse. Jack Kornfield reminds us to reference the practices of other cultures:

> In the Babemba tribe of South Africa, when a person acts irresponsibly or unjustly, he is placed in the center of the village, alone and unfettered. All work ceases, and every man, woman, and child in the village gathers in a large circle around the accused individual. Then each person in the tribe speaks to the accused, one at a time, each recalling the good things the person in the center of the circle has done in his lifetime. Every incident, every experience that can be recalled with any detail and accuracy, is recounted. All his positive attributes, good deeds, strengths, and kindnesses are recited carefully and at

length. This tribal ceremony often lasts for several days. At the end, the tribal circle is broken, a joyous celebration takes place, and the person is symbolically and literally welcomed back into the tribe (2004, 42).

_____

Note when you have received evaluations of your work. Have the negatives been balanced with positives? How do you think differently about your experiences when you do receive balanced feedback?

FOCUS ON THE PRESENT MOMENT

Education pushes out into the future as students are asked to master new content. Too often, we lose sight of the present and all those experiences we encounter in the here and now. Education becomes goal oriented, a matter of "hurdle jumping," and deeper possibilities are lost.

Tip 114. Offer a cup of tea

"When you are holding a cup of tea in your hand," insists Buddhist scholar and monk, Thich Nhat Hanh, "do it while being 100 percent there. You know how to do this—one deep in-breath, one gentle out-breath, and the body and mind come together. You are truly there, absolutely alive, fully present! This only takes ten or fifteen seconds, and suddenly the tea reveals itself to you in all its splendor and wonder....This is actually an offering of peace, of joy, and of concentration" (2009, 78).

Practice total concentration when you offer refreshments to others, whether in the classroom or out on the trail. Make it a time for peace and joy.

Tip 115. Know that Dewey was right! Model "Present-ness"

In *Teaching Community*, bell hooks advocates for education in the moment. "[Education] is so often geared toward the future, [and] the perceived awards that the imagined future will bring....In modern schooling the message students receive is that everything that they learn in the classroom is mere raw material for something that they will produce later in life. This displacement of meaning into the future makes it impossible for students to fully immerse themselves in the art of learning and to experience that immersion as a complete, satisfying moment of fulfillment" (2003, 165-166). bell hooks echoes John Dewey's thoughts about the ultimate goal of school. To paraphrase: school is life and not just preparation for life. By modeling this "present-ness" in your own actions and thoughts while teaching, you will be giving students a gift beyond the academic content.

Reflect on those classroom experiences when your learning was enhanced and deepened by your focus in the moment. List those factors that helped you focus. What can you do in an upcoming event to encourage this "present-ness"?

UTILIZE HISTORICAL PERSPECTIVES

Our past can teach so much about the future, from how we have arrived at this time and place and what has worked well to what has been problematic or disastrous. Past experiences become rich canvasses for analysis and evaluation, both personally and societally. As a testament to the power of historical knowledge, philosopher George Santayana's famous statement—*Those who cannot remember the past are condemned to repeat it*—dominates one wall of the museum that now occupies the buildings of the notorious Auschwitz concentration and death camp.

Tip 116. Feel your place in time

In her book, *Contemplative Hiking,* Margaret Emerson offers some ideas for deepening any experience out of doors. After hiking a trail on the Front Range of Colorado, she writes:

> One of the first things I noticed was the large amount of deer, elk, and coyote scat right there on the trail.... Despite the evidence, I didn't see one single deer or coyote while hiking, which made me wonder when these animals actually came out to hunt.... The scat was evidence of beings that exist somewhere, but are at the moment napping or hiding in their dens or foraging in more remote and private areas of the woods during the day. They are just out of reach and out of eyesight.
>
> Then there are the creatures that existed in a different moment in time, creatures that I know very little about and have never

Tip 119. Respond to individual and group diversity, seeing what we have in common

In *Teaching Diversity,* Timpson et al. describe the skills needed to allow individuals and groups to deepen their experiences together.

Understanding more about our differences allows us to make needed adjustments in any group. Practicing acceptance helps develop the trust needed for individuals to risk some vulnerability and open up to others and to possible change. Through their inherent diversity of membership—think broadly here and include background, personality, and disability—groups also provide an important challenge and opportunity for individuals to grow out of limiting assumptions and beliefs. The commitment of the group to inclusiveness provides the motivation to support individuals in their development. Unity around this kind of climate, along with a study of group dynamics and communication, provide the foundation needed by students to address diversity, fully explore their own differences and prejudices, and begin changing. (2003, 260)

In *147 Tips for Teaching Diversity,* Timpson et al. describe the range of ideas and approaches that can help address diversity issues in a group. Moreover, they also make a claim for us to understand what we have in common, what binds us to each other, insights that often emerge from experiential activities. "A preoccupation with differences can blind us to what we have in common. People can make huge leaps in overcoming prejudices and find acceptance when they realize that there are almost always greater differences *within* any group—height, weight, age, background, interests, abilities, motivations, etc.—than ever exist *between* groups that may differ along ethnic lines, gender, religious background, sexual orientation, etc." (2005, 17).

Holding a graduate class in a mountain retreat center in Colorado, Bill Timpson saw his group of doctoral students bond in new ways that cut across their traditional differences of ethnicity and gender. When the one smoker struggled at those high altitudes, two members of the group hung back, offering the support and assistance that she needed—and what everyone needed at some point—as we crossed swollen streams and searched for the disappearing path. When the hike on the second day evolved into an all day event, everyone found common ground in the shared memories and aching feet.

Assess the ability of participants to make the most of their experiences together:

- *their ability to accept each other even if they don't always agree with each other,*
- *to develop trust in each other,*
- *to risk some vulnerability,*
- *to open up to possible change,*
- *to grow out of limiting assumptions and beliefs,*
- *to be inclusive,*
- *to understand group dynamics, and*
- *to communicate effectively.*

Reflect on your experiences when diverse groups pulled together. Plan activities that will create common ground for future groups that you will lead.

Tip 120. Build gender awareness

Every culture reflects certain norms, traditions, and realities about the relationships between men and women. For example, in some countries unrelated men and women are forbidden to touch, or must have a chaperone present under certain circumstances when they meet. Gender dynamics should be considered when planning activities. Beliefs about gender roles could impact the learning you hope that takes place. These issues can be important when the classroom space opens up to more experiential learning. Diversity scholar bell hooks reminds us about the choices that people have: "Within in the patriarchal academy, women have consistently learned how to choose between the sexist biases in knowledge that reinscribe domination based on gender or the forms of knowledge that intensify awareness of gender equality and female self-determination" (2003, 2).

Identify past experiences when you noticed gender issues surfacing. Rethink an upcoming event to address any gender issues that you think might interfere with the learning that you hope will happen.

Tip 121. Provide diverse role models and focus on student success

Goldlin Wall has lived on and off the reservation. He has also worked with Native American Student Services at Colorado State University. He writes: "It is no coincidence Native Americans have struggled with education. Going from living a hard but simple life style to learning new ideas, philosophies, and values from mainstream American culture would make any one of us question the purpose of what is being taught. Consequently, an institutional support system can be vital for all students when they are trying to find their place. Native American students will often leave if that support system is not there." As Thompson reports, the "lack of models certainly contributes to the weaker motivation of Indian students and makes them potential dropouts" (1978, 80). Guillory and Wolverton (2008) conclude that US colleges and universities have struggled to adequately support Native American students in degree completion and Kleinfeld, Cooper, and Kyle agrees, insisting that "developing new strategies to increase the success of Native American students in college is an important challenge" (1987, 7).

Have institutions truly done everything to meet such a diverse group's needs? Consider scheduling a Native American speaker to offer a different kind of experience, recognizing that the different indigenous tribes, communities, and individuals will inevitably reflect a great diversity of perspectives.

Tip 122. Acknowledge and use adult experience

Those who work with adults may sometimes be tempted to teach in the same manner they remember being taught as children. This is understandable, since it is a common experience that occurs over and over again. However, adults are not the same as children. We need to acknowledge the wealth of experiences that adults have and how this will affect their learning. Merriam, Caffarella, and Baumgartner (2007) give a good summary of the affects experience can have on adult learning. They note 1) how adults can call on their experiences as resources for new learning; 2) how the need to make sense of life experiences may be an incentive for learning; 3) how adults use past experiences to transform meaning and values; and 4) how past experiences can also create barriers for new learning, such as having to unlearn old thinking or habits. Adults need to be treated like adults, and this means acknowledging the experiences they bring to learning, as well as using those experiences when designing activities.

Reflect on several experiences you have had that either encouraged you to learn or created a barrier to your learning. How could you determine what relevant experiences others bring?

DEVELOP
LEADERSHIP SKILLS

The very nature of activities opens up many possibilities for experiential learning about leadership and the skills that can help make group efforts more successful. Every meeting becomes an opportunity to experience something new or different, to reflect on what happened, what worked, and what could be improved.

Tip 123. Simultaneously stay on the balcony and on the dance floor

In *Leadership and Sustainability,* Michael Fullan draws on the published research about organizations and change to offer ideas for promoting enduring reform. Here he uses a metaphor to illustrate the principle of being fully engaged in the classroom while simultaneously staying alert to the bigger systems picture of the school or university. "The dance floor is the intense leadership for deep learning. The balcony is standing back to get perspective, and visiting other settings, where you can observe from a distance. Practice moving back and forth, being in the midst of the trees while you alternatively get a view of the whole forest" (2005, 103).

Find a forested area if you can. If you cannot, use your memory to recall a place where you have been before. Describe how this area looks from a distance. Now describe it when you are fully immersed and surrounded by it. Using this metaphor, draw from your experience to identify a problem area up close and a distance. List the insights that emerge.

Tip 124. Connect to your group's identity, the information you need, and each other

In her book, *Leadership and the New Science*, Meg Wheatley describes what is needed for any "system" to develop greater self knowledge. "People need to be connected to the fundamental *identity* of the organization or community. Who are we? Who do we aspire to become? How shall we be together? And people need to be connected to new *information*. What else do we need to know? Where is this new information to be found? And people need to be able to reach past traditional boundaries and develop *relationships* with people anywhere in the system. Who else needs to do this work with us?" (2001, 146).

Evaluate a group with whom you are connected on each of these three dimensions—identity, information, and relationships. Identify experiences that could make the group more effective.

Tip 125. Find a guide

Everyone could use a guide, especially during difficult or challenging experiences. Astin (1993) notes how college students, for example, often experience changes in attitude, behaviors, values, and personality, and that relationships and friendships can be keys to their success. Arum and Roksa remind us that along with friends and family, "another critical actor in the journey through higher education is faculty" (2011, 60).

Reflect on those experiences when you have had good guides and when you haven't, as well as those times when you were really on your own. Where could you find a good guide (mentor) for a challenging experience ahead? How could you a develop guides for the challenges you pose to your classes or audiences?

Tip 126. Use name games, ice breakers, and energizers

Ice breakers, name games, and energizers are activities that let people get to know each other, start simple conversations, encourage interaction, and set an open, accepting communication platform that helps to create a healthy learning environment. By taking a few moments to model open and sincere interactions, you can deepen the learning experience for everyone. The 'ice' that you are attempting to break can take many forms. People with different cultural, social, religious, or ethnic backgrounds may be unsure of how to join the group and what would be expected. When mixing people from different organizational and socio-economic backgrounds, there can be differences that might not "fit" everyone's style, personality, or preferences. "Breaking the ice" means using experiential tools to overcome inhibitions or worries, explore differences, and tap into the collective strengths of the group.

For example, one fun, energizing introduction activity is to have people introduce themselves as their favorite animal or vehicle and explain why. What people reveal about themselves helps both to build trust and support name recall. It can be important to tie the ice breaker into the specific needs that people have and/or to the activity or lesson you will be using. Keep in mind your intentions for the activity—open communication, comfort with contributing, teamwork—so that you can modify the activity as needed.

Reflect on your experience with ice breakers, name games, and energizers. List the potential benefits and suggest one to open your next session.

Tip 127. Develop self-leadership

When you facilitate learning, you are inherently a leader. How you choose to lead others can be a reflection on how you choose to lead yourself. Self-leadership represents the art and skill of knowing your origins, where you are now and where you want to go. Northouse (2010) outlines this form of critical self-assessment as part of the development of an authentic leadership style.

You can ask yourself:

- How have I developed my self-world view, i.e., my notion of self within my notion of the whole world?
- What basic or unnoticed assumptions do I have?

Be honest with where you are now. Ask yourself:

- What areas of myself am I afraid to engage or change?
- What areas of myself am I excited to change?
- How do I see the various roles (facilitator, learner) in the environment?
- What are my strengths and weaknesses in my ability to facilitate a learning experience?

- Do I really believe in the methods that I use, or have I become accustomed to facilitating in a certain manner?
- Is my method fully connecting with my students, exploring what is to be learned, and creating the highest potential for learning transfer?
- How is my self-world view coloring the design, facilitation, processing, and transfer of knowledge?

Be realistic about where you wish to go. Ask yourself:

- Have I set goals for my total development and not just for my skills as a facilitator?
- Have I sought out mentors to help me along the path.?

Be ready to engage in critical self-reflection when you facilitate learning. Practitioners who are not willing to reflect critically on their own practices will face problems.

Always allow space and time for yourself as a facilitator for learning to reflect critically on your own practice. Identify areas of effectiveness as well as areas where you need to grow.

PROMOTE ONGOING PROFESSIONAL DEVELOPMENT

Because of their isolation from each other in different self-contained classrooms, teachers and professors often need support and assistance to move in new directions. One or more people in the organization will need to value professional development enough to provide the needed resources and leadership.

Tip 128. Plan creatively and strategically for innovation

Innovative program planning requires creativity and effective and efficient use of resources, both human and financial. Curricula can be aligned with national and state standards while including varied experiences and opportunities for students—more creative use of the arts, engineering/technology projects, other exploratory electives, varied extra-curricular activities—but must be in alignment with a commitment from leaders who will work to create a sustainable organizational foundation. For example, clear benchmark outcomes are helpful so teachers and students can focus on whatever mastery is required. Yet, we also know that change can create anxieties, and we'll need to encourage everyone to be open-minded about a "new" culture of innovation. Fundamentally, there must be ongoing commitment by administration, faculty, staff, and community to excellence and to addressing the holistic needs of all students in every school system.

Examine your strategic plans for using experiential learning. What creativity can you add to encourage a climate of innovation?

Tip 129. Observe others and videotapes

In their classic text *Teaching Tips,* McKeachie and Svinicki make the case for experiential learning within professional development. Seeing yourself or others teaching can be a powerful mechanism for instructional improvement and innovation. "One of the best ways to learn a new skill is to see it performed. As you talk to your colleagues about teaching, ask if they would mind if you observed a class to see how they actually use a particular method. Faculty development centers frequently sponsor workshops in which you can see and experience particular methods of teaching or uses of technology. Videotapes demonstrating various methods of teaching are also available" (2006, 348).

Recall those times when you were able to learn much from observation of others. Develop a list of people you would like to observe and think through possibilities for creating a kind of internship for yourself. Seek out sources for videotaped demonstrations. Make a list and begin a schedule of observations, live and videotaped.

Tip 130. Align goals and values and commit to ongoing professional development

High quality programs that are experientially focused should have clear goals and values that both align with current educational research and prepare students for the rapidly changing world of the twenty-first century. In order to accomplish this, teachers should also make a commitment to ongoing professional development, as well as meaningful learning communities (Henderson and Milstein 2002; Fessler and Christensen 1991). Students should also be expected to become active members of those local, regional, national, and international associations that are most germane to their studies and future plans (Schön 1983).

Review a previous learning experience for its alignment of goals and values. Identify those organizations that would most help with sustaining this alignment and promoting ongoing professional development. Encourage students to become active in the professional organizations that define their fields of study.

Tip 131. Create a professional learning community

As one way to provide ongoing processing of experiences, an organization's staff could read and discuss articles, chapters, and books that speak to their workplace, product, or service. Incentives could be offered for useful ideas that emerge. Brief discussions could be held during announcements or other training sessions. Different staff could take responsibility for recommending readings, summarizing main points and leading the discussion about implications. Some kind of small reward or recognition could be given those presenting. Extended sessions could be added periodically for staff willing to *discuss and write* short responses to prompts about service or possible innovations. Former Uno Regional Vice President Jon Freedman remembers having "a reading series, Management 101. Presentations were assigned to general managers and culinary leads. Eventually it became fun. We read articles because they were more current and brief. Discussion questions were put out in advance." District General Manager Wade Moody adds: "There is so much value in reflection. I always feel like I'm learning. Every experience can be valuable. I often think back on how much better I could have been at this or that job with what I know now" (Guidara and Timpson, under development).

Create a professional learning community and develop a schedule of readings and responsibilities, dates and times. Be sure to debrief each session to assess its value and, what could be improved. Suggestions from Guidara and Timpson about interesting books included the following:

Bennis, Warren. 1989. *On Becoming a Leader.* New York: Basic Books/Perseus.

Blanchard, Kenneth and Spencer Johnson. 1981. *The One Minute Manager.* New York: William Morrow.

Collins, James. 2001. *Good to Great.* New York: HarperCollins.

Covey, Steven. 2004 *The 7 habits of highly effective people: Powerful lessons in personal change.* New York: Free Press.

Crum, Thomas. 1997. *Journey to Center: Lessons in Unifying Body, Mind and Spirit.* New York: Fireside.

Goleman, Daniel, Richard Boyatzis and Annie McKee. 2004. *Primal leadership: Learning to lead with emotional intelligence.*. Boston: Harvard Business School Press.

Guidara, Frank and William M. Timpson, under development. *What does your epitaph say? How teaching and learning can reinvigorate business.* Madison: Atwood Publishing.

Kurlansky, Mark 1998. *Cod: A Biography of the Fish that Changed the World.* New York: Penguin.

Kulansky, Mark. 2002. *Salt: A World History.* New York: Penguin.

Lawler, Edmund. 2001. *Lessons in Service from Charlie Trotter.* Berkeley, CA: Ten Speed Press.

Peters, Tom. 1987. *Thriving on Chaos: Handbook for Management Revolution.* New York: Knopf.

Stack, Jack. 1992. *The Great Game of Business.* New York: Bantam Doubleday.

APPLY EXPERIENTIAL LEARNING TO THE BUSINESS WORLD

People in business have often made use of the principles of experiential learning to better connect concepts and skills to their application and use. Learning cannot be left in the classroom.

Tip 132. Reserve judgment of others

In *Barnga©: A game on cultural clashes,* Khush Pittenger and Beverly Heimann introduced a game of cards in an Organizational Behavior class to discuss diversity management issues by simulating misperceptions that can arise due to subtle albeit potentially problematic cross cultural differences. The game may be played and debriefed in as little as 45 minutes, is interactive, and requires fairly minimal set-up time. "The participants experience cultural shock when they move from their group to another group who appears to be playing the same game but has different rules that they do not understand" (Pittenger and Heimann 1998, 253). The subtle differences encountered during the game highlight issues of mistrust, misjudgments, and problems in interpersonal relationships and task accomplishment. Participants are made aware of surface similarities and below-surface differences with people from other cultures who differ in the way they do things.

Consider learning situations you would like to explore in your organization. Plan ahead before conducting the game and debriefing the participants to develop a set of personalized discussion material. Sivasailam Thiagarajan (1990) suggested asking questions, such as: What experiences do you want to have in your next encounter with groups different from yourself? What can you do to increase the probability of having such experiences?

Tip 133. Reconcile differences between people

As a follow-up to Tip #132, know that *Barnga*© imposes a strict command of "no verbal communication" after the tournament commences. The misperceptions and consequent communication difficulties encountered during the game give rise to different feelings and reactions—frustration, success, ambiguity, uncertainty, and/or misunderstandings. The participants are challenged to bridge communication barriers and reconcile cross-cultural differences.

Help your staff realize that despite good intentions, people interpret things differently and often act accordingly. Plan a group follow-up discussion before conducting the game. Sivasailam Thiagarajan (1990) suggested asking questions such as: What does the game suggest about what to do when you are in a similar situation in the real world? What can you do to understand and resolve conflicts in order to function effectively with people from other cultures?

Tip 134. Understand yourself and others to manage people differences

In *People Styles at Work*, Robert Bolton and Dorothy Grover Bolton focused their attention on improving work relationships, although the concepts in their book can be applied in any setting. At the heart of their research is the premise that people can be grouped into four styles—Analyticals, Amiables, Expressives, and Drivers—based on their outer behaviors, which others can objectively identify fairly readily. The Boltons defined style as follows: "A person's style is his or her pattern of assertive and responsive behavior. The pattern is useful in predicting how the person prefers to work with others." (1996, 10) Your style is not based on how you see yourself, but rather how you are perceived by others. Self-assessment is the first step towards enhancing work relationships.

Complete and score the Behavioral Inventory as described by Bolton and Bolton (1996). Then, enhance your self-awareness by selecting three to five other trusted colleagues to take the inventory with reference to your behaviors and provide feedback.

Tip 135. Understand yourself and others to build more productive relationships

As a follow-up to Tip #134, Bolton and Grover Bolton argued that it is sometimes difficult to bridge gaps between different working styles; nonetheless, it is important to capitalize on differences between people who are important to your success and happiness. Common ground with people can be found by flexing to their style-based behavior patterns. "Style flex involves tailoring your behavior so the way you work fits better with the other person's style" (1996, 66). Style flex is neither manipulation nor conformity; it's temporarily adapting a few behaviors to better interact with someone.

Practice your style flex during a meeting. First determine the style-based differences between you and another person. Then adjust two or three types of behavior to more closely match those of that person. Notice any changes in your interactions.

Tip 136. Shake up ingrained perceptions to spark creativity

Some people assume novel ideas that lead to innovation are left to chance. However, there are those who have worked toward fostering creativity by adapting work environments and sharing information to allow new ideas to emerge. Maria Capozzi, Renée Dye, and Amy Howe (2011, 5) noted how leading neuroscientists have linked creativity intrinsically to perception. As a result, they discussed four practical ways to alter ingrained perceptions: 1) See and experience something first-hand outside the workplace, whether by purchasing your own product or service or visiting a competitor's place of business; 2) Identify and challenge core beliefs by asking questions such as, "What would customers *never* be willing to pay for?"; 3) Draw analogies; and 4) Impose artificial constraints. An example of making use of analogies to explore possible new business models involved asking a group of chief strategy officers (CSOs) from different organizations to imagine how Apple would design its retail formats. This question sparked a variety of ideas, one of which was considered by the retailer under study.

Consider your team members' implicit and explicit assumptions and their views of the world. What transformative experiences can you orchestrate that directly confront these deeply held beliefs? What questions can you tailor to spark creativity in your areas of interest?

Tip 137. Compose a sticky message to communicate effectively

Whether you are a CEO addressing the employees of your company or a teacher instructing students in your classroom, it is usually important to deliver your message as clearly and succinctly as possible. Equally important: make it memorable. In other words, communicate a message that sticks. In a July 2007 interview, Chip Heath suggested, "Leaders will spend weeks or months coming up with the right idea but then spend only a few hours thinking about how to convey that message to everybody else" (Mendonca and Miller 2007, 1). Stakeholders are asked to take action; employees are organized to rally behind an organization's mission; students are required to complete an assignment or take an exam. If you have an idea to convey, what message will you send and how will you elicit the desired response?

Consider messages you intend to deliver and decide which of them requires an action to be taken at some time in the future. Devote your efforts to design and communicate messages that need to persist over time. Make such messages simple by focusing on core elements; make them concrete by envisioning the less obvious that you often take for granted; and make them surprising through, for example, storytelling.

Tip 138. Build strategic muscle to succeed

Alina Waite noted, "Competition has become more intense and widespread in recent years" (2009, 333). As a result many organizations are challenged to be creative and innovative in order to stay ahead of their competition. Some leaders will take a short term approach and see only their direct competitors as threats in an ever changing business landscape rife with fierce rivals after their share of the worldwide market. To remain successful, however, these leaders need to take a longer term view and to expand their definition of competition to include indirect competitors as well (Porter 1998). It is realistic to think top management spends more time on strategy than ever before in order to cope with these increased pressures. Birshan and Kar suggested, "Involving more senior leaders in strategic dialogue makes it easier to stay ahead of emerging opportunities, respond quickly to unexpected threats, and make timely decisions" (2012, 1).

Yet, many who rise up the ranks are ill equipped to develop strategies. Birshan and Kar offer three tips to build strategic muscle: 1) Know thy industry, the very context in which your organization is situated; 2) Identify potential disrupters by continually gaining competitive insights; 3) Take a disciplined approach to facilitate communication. Birshan and Kar report that an experiential exercise once led board members to arrange samples of men's boxer shorts, minus their labels, "in order of price so they could see how their perceptions of quality were driven by brands and not manufacturing standards" (2012, 7).

Consider taking your team on an experiential excursion off-site to see your industry from an alternate vantage point and away from all the cues that dominate the place where people work every day. Lead an experiential exercise drawn from this book to allow your team to think strategically and communicate effectively.

STUDY CHANGE AND FACE THE FUTURE

Those who study change tend to be better at navigating its challenges. You understand more about the inherent complexities and ambiguities involved in change and what the emotional requirements might be. Being in denial of what needs to change benefits no one.

Tip 139. Understand change and take action

There are more and more signs of environmental damage to the air we breathe, the water we can get, the declining stocks of fish and dead zones in our oceans, global warming, and climate change generally. The world faces a crisis on many fronts as populations continue to grow and our appetite for industrial products threatens the very carrying capacity of the earth itself. We have every reason to change the ways in which we think and act.

In *147 Tips for Teaching Peace and Reconciliation*, Timpson et al. describe the importance of understanding change when we try to find peaceful ways through conflict, reduce violence, and avoid war. "Scholars of change—Seymour Sarason and Michael Fullan are two of the most cited in educational circles—seem to agree that to be successful, people need to understand the dynamics of change, where and how it can be derailed, and where and how to focus energies and talents....You can also study the lessons of history—how people fostered change (2009, 139)." With respect to peace and reconciliation, we think of Mahatma Gandhi, Nelson Mandela, Bishop Desmond Tutu, Martin Luther King, Jr., Rosa Parks, Maya Angelou, bell hooks, Chief Seattle, Eleanor Roosevelt, and others.

Learn about action research that intends to study and improve practice locally and get involved in a change project in your community. Create a service learning assignment for students in your classes or members of your audience. Make a list of those change agents who have been important to you.

Tip 140. Connect your experiences with future challenges

Because the future is an unknown, everyone will need more than information to navigate its surprises, setbacks, and twists and turns. Experiential learning can reveal valuable parts of ourselves that might otherwise remain inaccessible. In his book, *Enough,* Bill McKibben takes on the complex topic of technology and its impact on our lives, both now and in the future, and how his personal experiences affected his thinking. For example, running a marathon raised McKibbon's awareness about his own strengths and limitations.

> For a period of hours, and especially those last gritty miles, I had been absolutely, utterly *present,* the moments desperately, magnificently clarified. As meaningless as it was to the world, that's how meaningful it was to me. I met parts of myself I'd never been introduced to before, glimpsed more clearly strengths and flaws I'd half suspected. A marathon peels you down toward your core for a little while, gets past the defenses we erect even against ourselves.... And yet it is entirely possible that we will be among the last generations to feel that power and that frailty. Genetic science may soon offer human beings, among many other things, the power to bless their offspring with a vastly improved engine. For instance, scientists may find ways to dramatically increase the amount of oxygen that blood can carry. When that happens, we will...be able to run and not grow weary. (2003, 2-3)

Reflect on experiences you have had that revealed otherwise unknown parts of yourself. List ways in which you could rethink an upcoming presentation to include this kind of personal insight.

Tip 141. Know the "bottom line" and think like an ecologist

Whatever the arguments for or against climate change, looking at experience, at the data, suggests a "both-and" argument when you ask about the role of business—that is, contributing to the problem and helping with various solutions. In *Getting Green Done,* Auden Schendler, Vice President of Sustainability at Aspen Skiing Company, offers the following:

> Business is both the cause and the victim of environmental decline. Good example: The Chilean sea bass I saw on the menu at a restaurant recently. It will be commercially extinct in two years. Then what do restaurants serve? Better example: At our ski resorts, we will have to make more and more snow to stay in business in a warming climate, which costs us more and more money and uses more and more energy, which in turn warms the climate, requiring us to make more snow. We are cannibalizing the climate we depend on to stay in business, eating our own tail to stay alive. Climate change threatens every business on the planet, and business is the primary cause of it. As a result, more and more companies...are seeking ways to operate without hurting the environment. They are doing this because of the obvious threat, but they also anticipate a growing desire among consumers for 'green' products and services. Equally important, if business is in large part the cause of the planet's problems, then it can also be the solution. (2009, 6)

In *The Ten Minute Ecologist,* John Janovy makes the case for all of us understanding more about the natural world, especially since computers, televisions and other technologies dominate more and more of our work and personal lives.

> In the not-too-distant past, human products were primarily art, music, literature, machines, and buildings—relatively long-lived, tangible items. Recently, however, human products have come to include electronic images and sounds, which bear only a superficial resemblance to anything alive. These images and sounds can be manipulated in uncountable ways, and the results are often quite seductive for humans, who are, by definition, very intelligent animals who use their imaginations and often seek mental stimulation.

We have thus generated a philosophical problem: whether our electronic images are 'real.' The answer is relatively simple 'yes.' Images are real. But (this is a fairly large 'but') these are very real images. Real in the philosophical sense may have absolutely no connection with any of the natural processes that support life on Earth, and indeed may convince us that we've successfully separated ourselves from these processes....Between these two extremes lies a vast territory of human thought, action, and rationale. Somewhere in that territory stands the ecologist, who believes that humans must act wisely in their relationships with Earth. And the more tightly human perception is governed by knowledge of the planet, claims the ecologist, the better the future looks for all of us. (1997, 4-5)

Identify other examples where experiences defined the problem and new thinking suggested possible solutions. Identify the times when you have thought and acted like an ecologist. What experiences or activities could help people better connect to a deeper knowledge of the planet? List what you could add to an upcoming presentation or activity.

Tip 142. Counteract "bureaucratic" complicity and group inertia

Given our traditional preoccupation with reductionist theories and memorized knowledge, our classrooms can become quite disconnected from the messy complexities of the real world. In her book, *Finding Beauty in a Broken World,* Terry Tempest Williams describes her experiences in Rwanda helping an artist create, with broken pieces of pottery, mosaic memorials to the genocide of 1994. "The word 'genocide' first appeared in print by the Jewish scholar, Raphael Lemkin in his book *Axis Rule in Occupied Europe,* published in 1944. But the word did not take hold until after the Holocaust. Lemkin finally persuaded the United Nations General Assembly to adopt an internationally accepted definition of genocide crafted during the Convention on the Prevention and Punishment of the Crime of Genocide, on December 9, 1948" (2009, 238).

Beyond knowing the origins of the concept of genocide, it took Williams' experiences in Rwanda and direct evidence of that slaughter of 800,000 people, mostly Tutsi, a legacy of colonial imposed division and hierarchy, to reinforce the problem that she could see in excessive "bureaucratic" debate and discussion. "The masterminds of all genocides count on our complicity. They plan, calculate, and execute their intent, trusting in our refusal to acknowledge what they are doing. And in the case of America, instead of intervention, our government debated for months whether the killings in Rwanda fulfilled the definition of genocide. The manipulation of extinction is done most efficiently through bureaucracies" (2009, 239).

When has direct experience given you insights that would not have come through debate or discussion? List how you could use visits to the field to enrich an upcoming discussion and deepen learning.

Tip 143. Use the "Four F's": Flying fingers, Facebook and frustration.

Eden Haywood-Bird, an early childhood specialist, sees much potential in the use of newer social networking technology for learning, how students and instructors could be in much greater contact when out in the field, for example. She writes: "We can see the younger generation communicating differently and that this can cause problems or open up new possibilities for instructors. Just as older generations where at odds with their elders over the phone calls that often replaced written letters, we now see students who routinely communicate through text messaging, email, Twitter, and Facebook during class." Haywood-Bird cites a study by Duran et al. (2005) that showed an increase in perceived positive interactions among both faculty and students when email was utilized more by instructors. "Flying fingers and Facebook" can cause frustrations in class when instructors want students to focus, but there is also the potential for increased and creative interactions both in and out of class.

Accept that others may interact differently with the world than you do. Connecting more with students with new technologies can deepen your relationship with them both in and out of class. Consult with others who are making good and creative use of these new social network technologies. Rethink an upcoming class or course and explore ways in which you could make greater use of Facebook, Twitter, or other new communication technologies. Make a list of what you will implement, even if only on a trail basis.

TEACH MINDFULNESS AND NURTURE CONSCIOUS AWARENESS

Meditation is a well studied means for focusing attention, reducing stress, increasing insight, and promoting creativity. Mindfulness and increased awareness are central foci for experiential learning, ways to break through the paradigms we are taught, the concepts that we learn in school and other organizations that define the way we see the world. Mindfulness practices (meditation) help keep us present. Awareness raising activities help deconstruct the taught mindset, allowing us to see the world differently. For example, "taught" by parents, the community, religious leaders and the scholars of the day that the world was the center of the universe, Galileo used his direct experience of watching the stars and the planets to challenge that notion that the earth was the center of our universe and to suggest, against great opposition and threats of recrimination, that the earth, in truth, rotated around the sun. Meditation is a discipline that can help calm the "busyness" of the brain, the constant flood of messages and input from the world and its latest technologies. A regular practice can help find that deeper meaning within an activity.

Tip 144. Use meditation to deepen understanding

Whether focusing on our breath in meditation or completing an individual experience out in the wilds, coming to understand what is underneath our reactions, fears, and assumptions will open us up to new insights and deeper learning. In her book on meditation, *Real Happiness,* Buddhist teacher Sharon Salzberg (2011b) connects the daily practice of meditation with a more centered and clear view of our own stuff—our fears and hopes, concerns and frustrations—what is really going on all around us, and how the reality of change undermines our perceived need for security, comfort, and our own spin on the world. Especially important is her analysis of assumptions, how our perceptions of others color our actions and interactions—the kids we like and don't like, the colleagues who push our buttons, those above who make us jump and the ones we so want to please, even the friends who disappoint us. It seems that we are always projecting our needs, fears, and concerns onto others and seeing what we want to see. In another publication, she writes:

> Meditation lets us be discerning in our dealings with the world, responsive in our intimate relationships, and honest when we examine our own feelings and motives. Attention determines our degree of intimacy with our ordinary experiences and contours our entire sense of connection to life (2011a, 51-52).

And so it is with our beliefs, she insists:

> [Our] assumptions keep us from appreciating what's right in front of us—a stranger who's a potential friend, a perceived adversary who might actually be a source of help. Assumptions block direct experience and prevent us from gathering information that could bring us comfort and relief, or information that, though saddening and painful, will allow us to make better decisions (2011a, 53).

Practice meditating before an upcoming presentation. Use the same centering principles for reflecting on recent experiences and seeking deeper insights. Make notes to yourself as reminders.

Tip 145. Raise awareness about life and potential change

Experiential learning begins with awareness, of the setting and of ourselves. Many activities have been developed to simulate a disability, for example, in the expectation that temporarily going without sight or using a wheelchair will have a bigger impact than just reading about that form of disability. With a greater awareness will hopefully come a deeper understanding and sensitivity to the challenges people face. With this kind of experience, we can become better advocates for needed changes.

Experiential learning can heighten this awareness. In *You Are Here*, Buddhist monk and peace advocate Thich Nhat Hanh describes the importance of this kind of "body awareness" and how this links with the reality of the physical changes we all must accept and understand.

> We need to learn to see our physical form as a river. Our body is not a static thing—it changes all the time. It is very important to see our physical form as something impermanent, as a river that is constantly changing. Every cell in our body is a drop of water in that river. Birth and death are happening continuously, in every moment of our daily lives. We must live every moment with death and life present at the same time. Both death and life are happening every moment in the river of our physical body. We should train ourselves in this vision of impermanence. (2009, 27)

Standing on top of a telephone pole on a Ropes/Challenge course, trying to keep shaky knees from buckling and preparing to leap for a trapeze several feet away, can remind every participant about that powerful force that warns us of danger and reminds us of life.

Reflect on those memories that are most vivid, that touch into your awareness of a deeper life force and the need for some changes. List ways in which this "body awareness" could lead you toward change in the future.

Tip 146. Wake up to the here and now

The benefits of experiential learning become more real when we can escape the dominant instructional paradigm of memorizing knowledge for future testing. In *Awakening Loving Kindness*, Pema Chödrön makes the argument for meditation as a discipline that can help us wake up to what we face in the present. "It's very helpful to realize that being here, sitting in meditation, doing simple everyday things like working, walking outside, talking with people, bathing, using the toilet, and eating, is actually all that we need to be fully awake, fully alive, fully human....Furthermore, the emotions that we have right now, the negativity and the positivity, are what we actually need. It is just as if we had looked around to find out what would be the greatest wealth that we could possibly possess in order to lead a decent, good, completely fulfilling, energetic, inspired life, and found it all right here" (1996, 8-9).

Whenever we are outside the traditional classroom and learning more from our experiences, we are forced into doing more with our own reactions, thoughts, and feelings. Amidst all the interpretations, advice, and input we may get from others, Buddhist teacher and writer Pema Chödrön encourages us to hold on to our own principles.

'Of the two witnesses, hold the principal one' is saying that one witness is everybody else giving you their feedback and opinions (which is worth listening to; there's some truth in what people say), but the principal witness is yourself. You're the only one who knows when you're opening and when you're closing. You're the only one who knows when you're using things to protect yourself and keep your ego together and when you're opening and letting things fall apart, letting the world come as it is—working with it rather than struggling against it. You're the only one who knows. (2001, 89)

Identify those aspects of your daily life that can be fulfilling, energizing, and inspiring. Make a list of new priorities that emphasize what is more meaningful. Evaluate your learning outside of formal classrooms. When have you held firm to your own principles even when these were different from those around you? When have you given in to the feedback and opinions of others? What promises can you make to yourself about an upcoming event?

Tip 147. Concentrate on the miracle in front of you, use a journal and silence

Buddhist author and monk Thich Nhat Hanh draws on his meditation practice to make the most of every moment. He writes: "Concentration is the practice of happiness. There is no happiness without concentration. When you eat an orange, try to practice concentration. Eat in such a way that pleasure, joy, and happiness are possible the whole time. You could call this orange meditation. You take an orange in the palm of your hand. You look at it and breathe in such a way that it reveals itself as the miracle it is. An orange is nothing less than a miracle. It is just like you—you are also a miracle of life" (2009, 79-80).

In *It's Up To You,* Dzigar Kongtrül, a Tibetan lama who has taught at Naropa University and now heads up retreat centers in Colorado and Vermont, describes the various ways in which meditation and self-reflection can add clarity to our experiences in life. He writes: "The point of the practice of self-reflection is to experience things clearly, without muddying the water by trying to change or control them" (2006, 13).

Silent moments in a classroom or meeting may seem like silent hours. "It is not uncommon to be threatened by silences to the point that we frequently do something counterproductive to break the silence and thus relieve our anxiety" (Corey 1996, 35) Silence can have several outcomes: we can process our experiences; we can also communicate with others without words. Silence can be refreshing or overwhelming. When silence does occur, we can avoid rushing in to fill that space, but, instead, acknowledge it, share our feelings about it, and then discuss its meaning and impact on the group or the experience we are trying to understand.

Silence can even be cultural. In *Articulate Silences,* King-Kok Cheung emphasizes that this privileging of speaking over silence is Eurocentric, which she sees "as polarized, hierarchical and gendered" (1993, 23) and notes that it is "not just prohibition against speech but also coercion to speak [that] can block articulation" (1993, 169). She notes "the fact that silence, too, can speak many tongues, varying from culture to culture" (1993, 1).

Commit to practicing a form of concentration whenever you eat, if only for a few moments. Learn to appreciate the miracle of your food, how it draws on the sun and the earth to grow from seed to maturity. Identify what you can do to appreciate the miracle of learning in your classes, presentations, and activities. Make a commitment to sit quietly when you want to make sense of recent experiences, especially those that are intense, frustrating, or conflicted. You can also use journal writing as an experience in silence. Commit to debriefing after an activity so participants can share reactions and insights.

Think back to those times when silence allowed for deeper insights or when a rush to fill a space with words precluded a deeper possibility. Make some notes about what you could do to create and use moments of silence in your classes, meetings or presentations.

REFERENCES

Alberti, Robert, and Michael Emmons. 2008. *Your perfect right: Assertiveness and equality in your life and relationships.* 9th ed. Atascadero, CA: Impact.

Albom, Mitch. 1997. *Tuesdays with Morrie: An old man, a young man, and life's greatest lesson.* New York: Doubleday/Random House.

Apple, Michael, and James Beane. 1995. *Democratic schools.* Portsmouth, NH: Heinemann.

Arum, Richard, and Josipa Roksa. 2011. *Academically adrift: Limited learning on college campuses.* Chicago: University of Chicago Press.

Astin, Alexander W. 1993. What matters in college: Four critical years revisited. *Liberal Education.* 79(4) (Fall 1993): 4-12.

Ausubel, David P. 1967. *The psychology of meaningful verbal learning.* New York: Grune & Stratton.

Bacon, Stephen B. 1983. *The conscious use of metaphor in outward bound.* Denver, CO: Colorado Outward Bound School.

Barnes, Louis, C. Roland Christensen, and Abby Hansen. 1994. *Teaching and the case study method.* 3rd ed. Boston: Harvard Business Press.

Barrows, Howard S., and Robyn M. Tamblyn. 1980. *Problem-based learning: An approach to medical education.* New York: Springer Publishing.

Berne, Eric. 1964. *Games people play: The psychology of human relations.* New York: Grove Press.

Bloom, Benjamin S., M. D. Engelhart, E. J. Furst, W. H. Hill, and D. R. Krathwohl. 1956. *Taxonomy of educational objectives: The classification of educational goals: Handbook I, Cognitive domain.* New York: Longman.

Bloom, Benjamin. 1973. *Every kid can: Learning for mastery.* Washington, DC: College University Press.

Birshan, Michael, and Jayanti Kar. July, 2012. Becoming more strategic: Three tips for any executive. *McKinsey Quarterly.* http://www.mckinseyquarterly.com/Becoming_more_strategic_Three_tips_for_any_executive_2992 (accessed July 19, 2012)

Bohm, David. 1980. *Wholeness and the implicate order.* New York: Routledge.

Bolton, Robert, and Dorothy Grover Bolton. 1996. *People styles at work: Making bad relationships good and good relationship better.* New York: AMACOM.

Book of Readings. 1990(?). Portland OR: Pacific Crest Outward Bound School.

Brandes, Gabriella, and Natasha Boskic. 2008. EPortfolios: From description to analysis. *International Review of Research in Open and Distance Learning.* 9(2): 1-17.

Brookfield, Stephen. 2005. *The power of critical theory: Liberating adult learning and teaching.* San Francisco: Jossey-Bass/John Wiley.

Brown, Terry J. 1999. Adventure risk management. In *Adventure Programming.* John C. Miles and Simon Priest, ed. State College, PA: Venture Publishing. 273-283.

Bruner, Jerome, Jacqueline Goodnow, and George Austin. 1967. *A study of thinking.* New York: Science Editions.

Bruner, Jerome. S. 1975. The ontogenesis of speech acts. *Journal of Child Language.* 2: 1-40.

Caffarella, Rosemary S. 2002. *Planning programs for adult learners: A practical guide for educators, trainers, and staff developers.* San Francisco: Jossey-Bass.

Callahan, Aimee, Elizabeth Erichsen, Leann M. R. Kaiser, and Kelsee Miller. 2009. Our quest: How we negotiate our multiple selves on a daily basis. *Journal of Adult Education.* 38(2):1-18.

Capozzi, Maria M., Renée Dye, and Amy Howe. April, 2011. Sparking creativity in teams: An executive's guide. *McKinsey Quarterly.* Http://www.mckinseyquarterly.com/ Sparking_creativity_in_teams_An_executives_guide_2786 (accessed July 19, 2012)

Carroll, John B. 1963. A model of school learning. *Teachers College Record.* 64(8):723-733.

Carroll, Michael. 2008. *The mindful leader.* Boston: Trumpeter Books.

Cheung, King-Kok. 1993. *Articulate silences: Hisaye Yamamoto, Maxine Hong Kingston and Joy Kogewa.* Ithaca, NY: Cornell University Press.

Chödrön, Pema. 1996. *Awakening loving kindness.* Boston: Shambhala.

_____. 1997. *When things fall apart: Heart advice for difficult times.* Boston: Shambhala.

_____. 2001a. *The places that scare you: A guide to fearlessness in difficult times.* Boston: Shambhala.

_____. 2001b. *Start where you are: A guide to compassionate living.* Boston: Shambhala.

_____. 2006. *Practicing peace in times of war.* Boston: Shambhala.

Collins, James. 2001. *Good to great.* New York: HarperCollins.

Corey, Gerald. 2013. *Theory and practice of counseling and psychotherapy.* 5th ed. Pacific Grove, CA: Brooks/Cole.

Covey, Steven. 2004. *The 7 habits of highly effective people: Powerful lessons in personal change.* New York: Free Press.

Csikszenthmihalyi, Mihaly. 1990. *Flow.* New York: Harper Collins.

Davis, Barbara Gross. 1993. *Tools for teaching*. San Francisco: Jossey-Bass.

Dewey, John. 1938. *Experience & education*. New York: Touchstone.

Dörnyei, Zoltán. 2001. *Teaching and researching motivation*. Harlow, UK: Pearson Education Limited.

Duran, Robert L., Lynne Kelly, and James A. Keaten. 2005. College faculty use and perceptions of electronic mail to communicate with students. *Communication Quarterly*. 53(2): 159-176.

Egan, Kieran. 2005. *An imaginative approach to teaching*. San Francisco: Jossey-Bass

Emerson, Margaret. 2010. *Contemplative hiking along the Colorado front range*. Broomfield, CO: Images and Adjectives.

Ennis, Catherine D., and M. Terri McCauley. 2002. Creating urban classroom communities worthy of trust. *Journal of Curriculum Studies*. 34(2): 149-172.

Fessler, Ralph, and Judith Christensen. 1991. *The teacher career cycle: Understanding and guiding the professional development of teachers*. Boston: Allyn & Bacon.

Flick, Deborah. 1998. *From debate to dialogue: Using the understanding process to transform our conversations*. Boulder: Orchid Publications.

Freire, Paulo. 1970. *Pedagogy of the oppressed*. New York: Continuum.

Fullan, Michael. 2005. *Leadership and sustainability: System thinkers in action*. Thousand Oaks, CA: Corwin.

Gage, Nathanial, and David Berliner. 1998. *Educational psychology*. Boston: Houghton Mifflin.

Galbraith, Michael W. 2004. *Adult learning methods: A guide for effective instruction*. Malibar, FL: Krieger.

Gardner, Howard. 1983. *Frames of mind: The theory of multiple intelligences*. New York: Basic Books.

_____. 1999. *Intelligence reframed: Multiple intelligences for the 21st century*. New York: Basic Books.

_____. 2000. *The disciplined mind: Beyond facts and standardized tests. The K-12 education that every child deserves*. New York: Penguin.

Gardner, Robert C. 1985. *Social Psychology and second language learning: The role of attitudes and motivation*. Baltimore, MD: Edward Arnold.

Garrick, Lora, and Haworth, Bob. 2001. *Readings—Colorado outward bound school, 40th Anniversary Edition*. Denver, CO: Hotchkiss, Inc.

Giaconia, Rose. 1987. Teacher questioning and wait-time. PhD diss., Stanford University, CA.

Gilligan, Carol. 1993. *In a different voice: Psychological Theory and Women's Development*. Cambridge: Harvard University Press.

Gimian, Carolyn Rose, ed. 2008. *The Pocket Chögyam Trungpa*. Boston: Shambhala.

Gladwell, Malcolm. 2000. *The tipping point: How little things can make a big difference*. New York: Little, Brown, and Company.

157

Goleman, Daniel, Richard Boyatzis, and Annie McKee. 2004. *Primal leadership: Learning to lead with emotional intelligence.* Boston: Harvard Business School Press.

Goleman, Daniel. 2009. *Ecological intelligence: How knowing the hidden impacts of what we buy can change everything.* New York: Broadway Books.

Grim, Frédérique. 2010. "Giving Authentic Opportunities to Second Language Learners: A look at a French Service-Learning Project." *Foreign Language Annals.* 43(4): 605-623.

Guidara, Frank, and William Timpson. Under development. *What does your epitaph say? How teaching and learning can reinvigorate business.* Madison: Atwood Publishing.

Guillory, Ralphael, and Mimi Wolverton. 2008. It's about family: Native Americans student persistence in higher education. *The Journal of Higher Education.* 79(1): 58-87.

Gunn, Angus, Robert Richburg, and Rita Smilkstein. (2007) *Igniting student potential: Teaching with the brain's natural learning process.* Thousand Oaks, CA: Corwin.

Hanh, Thich Nhat. 2009. *You are here: Discovering the magic of the present moment.* Boston: Shambhala.

Heider, John. 1985. *The Tao of leadership: Lao Tzu's Tao Te Ching adapted for a new age.* Atlanta, GA: Humanics Limited.

Helgesen, Sally. 1995. *The web of inclusion.* New York: Doubleday.

Henderson, Nan, and Mike Milstein. 2002. *Resiliency in schools: Making it happen for students and educators.* Thousand Oaks, CA: Corwin Press.

hooks, bell. 2003. *Teaching community: A pedagogy of hope.* New York: Henry Holt.

Itin, C. M. 1999. Reasserting the Philosophy of Experiential Education as a Vehicle for Change in the 21st Century. *The Journal of Experiential Education.* 22(2): 91-98.

Jacobs, Ed E., Robert L. Masson, Riley L. Harvill, and Christine J. Schimmel. 2009. *Group counseling: Strategies and skills.* 7th ed. Belmont, CA: Brooks/Cole.

Janovy, John, Jr. 1997. *10 minute ecologist: 20 answered questions for busy people facing environmental issues.* New York: St. Martin's Press.

Jackson, Wes. 1994. *Becoming native to this place.* Washington, DC: Counterpoint.

Johnson, David, and Roger Johnson. 1998. *Learning together and alone.* Boston: Allyn and Bacon.

Kaiser, Leann, and Elizabeth Erichsen. 2012. Narrative tools for facilitating research and learning for transformation. In *Pathways to transformation: Learning in relationship.* Carrie J. Boden McGill and Sola M. Kippers, ed. Charlotte, NC: Information Age Publishing. 49-64.

Kaminski, Karen, Jeffrey M. Foley and Leann M. R. Kaiser. 2013. *Applying Transfer in Practice. In Learning Transfer in Adult Education: New Directions for Adult and Continuing Education, Number 137.* Leann M. R. Kaiser, Karen Kaminski and Jeffrey M. Foley, ed. San Francisco: Jossey-Bass. 83-89.

Kolb, David. 1984. *Experiential learning.* Upper Saddle River, NJ: Prentice Hall.

Kamkwamba, William and Bryan Mealer. 2009. *The boy who harnessed the wind: Creating currents of electricity and hope*. New York: Harper.

Kleinfeld, Judith, Joe Cooper, and Nathan Kyle. 1987. Postsecondary Counselors: A model for increasing Native Americans' college success. *Journal of American Indian Education*. 27(1): 9-16.

Knowles, Malcolm S., Elwood F. Holton, and Richard A. Swanson. 2011. *The adult learner: the definitive classic in adult education and human resource development*. 7th ed. Burlington, MA: Elsevier.

Kohlberg, Lawrence. 1963. The development of children's orientation toward moral order: Sequence in the development of moral thought. *Vita Humana* 6:11-33.

Kongtrül, Dzigar. 2005. *It's up to you: The practice of self-reflection on the Buddhist path*. Boston: Shambhala.

Kornfield, Jack. 2004. *The art of forgiveness, loving kindness, and peace*. New York: Bantam.

Land, George, and Beth Jarman. 1992. *Break point and beyond*. New York: NY: Harper Business.

Lawler, Edmund. 2001. *Lessons in service from Charlie Trotter*. Berkeley, CA: Ten Speed Press.

Louv, Richard. 2008. *Last child in the woods: Saving our children from nature-deficit disorder*. Chapel Hill, NC: Algonquin Books.

Lowman, Joseph. 1995. *Mastering the techniques of teaching*. San Francisco: Jossey-Bass.

Lui, Xiaojing, Richard J. Magjuka, Curtis J. Bonk, and Seuge-hee Lee. 2007. Does a sense of community matter? An examination of participants' perceptions of building learning communities in online courses. *The Quarterly Review of Distance Education*. 8(1): 9-24.

Mager, Robert F. 1997. *How to turn learners on . . . without turning them off: Ways to ignite interest in learning*. 3rd ed. Atlanta, GA: Center for Effective Performance.

McClelland, David. 1985. *Human motivation*. Glenview, IL: Scott Foresman.

McKeachie, Wilbert, and Marilla Svinicki. 2006. *McKeachie's Teaching tips: Strategies, research, and theory for college and university teachers*. 12th ed. Boston: Houghton Mifflin.

McKibben, William. 2003. *Enough: Staying human in an engineered age*. New York, NY: Henry Holt.

Mendonca, Lenny T., and Matt Miller. November, 2007. Crafting a message that sticks: An interview with Chip Heath. *McKinsey Quarterly*. http://www.mckinseyquarterly.com/Crafting_a_message_that_sticks_An_interview_with_Chip_Heath_2062 (accessed July 19, 2012).

Merriam, Sharan B., Rosemary S. Caffarella, and Lisa M. Baumgartner. 2006. *Learning in adulthood: A comprehensive guide*. 3rd ed. San Francisco: Jossey-Bass.

Middleton, Val. 2003. Reaching the congregation, not just the choir. In *Teaching diversity: Challenges and complexities, identities and integrity*. William M. Timpson,

Silvia Sara Canetto, Evelinn Borrayo, and Raymond Yang, ed. Madison: Atwood Publishing. 103-115.

Miller, George. 1956. The magical number seven, plus or minus two: Some limits on our capacities for processing information. *Psychological Review*. 63(2): 81-97.

Mipham, Sakyong. 2003. *Turning the mind into an ally*. New York: Riverhead.

Northouse, Peter. 2010. *Leadership theory and practice*. 5th ed. Thousand Oaks, CA: Sage.

Ormrod, Jeanne Ellis. 1998. *Educational psychology: Developing learners*. 2nd ed. Upper Saddle River, NJ: Prentice Hall.

Orr, David W. 1994. *Earth in mind: On education, environment, and the human prospect*. Washington, DC: Island Press.

Orr, David W. 2004. *The last refuge: Patriotism, politics, and the environment in an age of terror*. Washington, DC: Island Press.

Palmer, Parker. 1998. *The courage to teach: Exploring the inner landscape of a teacher's life*. San Francisco: Jossey-Bass.

Patrick, Catharine. 1955. *What is creative thinking?* New York: Philosophical Library.

Pausch, Randy. 2008. *The last lecture*. New York: Hyperion.

Perry, William G., Jr. 1981. Cognitive and ethical growth: The making of meaning. In *The modern American college*, Arthur W. Chickering and Associates, ed. San Francisco: Jossey-Bass. 76-116.

Perry, William G., Jr. 1999. *Forms of intellectual and ethical development in the college years: A scheme*. San Francisco: Jossey-Bass.

Piaget, Jean. 1952. *The origins of intelligence in children*. Margaret Cook, trans. New York: International University Press.

Piaget, Jean. 1970. *The science of education and the psychology of the child*. New York: Orion.

Pittenger, Khush K., and Beverly Heimann. 1998. Barnga®: A game on cultural clashes. In *Developments in Business Simulation & Experiential Learning Conference*. Vol. 25. Proceedings of ABSEL conference, Jan. 1998. Nancy H. Leonard and Sandra W. Morgan, ed. Madison, WI: Omnipress. 253-254.

Porter, Michael E. 1998. *On competition*. Boston: Harvard Business School Publishing.

Priest, Simon, and Michael A. Gass. 2005. *Effective leadership in adventure programming*. 2nd ed. Champaign, IL: Human Kinetics.

Ramsden, Paul. 1992. *Learning to teach in higher education*. New York: Routledge.

Rohnke, Karl. 1989. *Cowstails and cobras II: A guide to games, initiatives, ropes courses and adventure curriculum*. Dubuque, IA: Kendall Hunt.

Rosenberg, Marshall. 2002. *Nonviolent communication: The Language of Life*. Encinitas, CA: PuddleDancer Press.

Rowe, Mary Budd. 1974. Wait-time and rewards as instructional variables, their influence on language, logic, and fate control: Part one—wait time. *Journal of Research in Science Teaching*. 11(2): 81-94.

Salzberg, Sharon. 2011a. Real happiness. (Excerpt from *Real happiness: The power of meditation: A 28 day program*). *Shambhala Sun*. May 2011: 51-54, 89-90.

Salzberg, Sharon. 2011b. *Real happiness: The power of meditation: A 28 day program*. New York: Workman Publishing.

Schatz, Mona. 2003. Using dialogue discussion groups when addressing sensitive topics. In *Teaching diversity: Challenges and complexities, identities and integrity*. William M. Timpson, Silvia Sara Canetto, Evelinn Borrayo, and Raymond Yang, ed. Madison, WI: Atwood Publishing. 117-132.

Schendler, Auden. 2009. *Getting green done: Hard truths from the front lines of the sustainability revolution*. New York: Public Affairs.

Schön, Donald. 1983. *The reflective practitioner: How professionals think in action*. (New York?): Basic Books.

Senge, Peter. 1990. *The fifth discipline: The art and practice of the learning organization*. New York: Currency/Doubleday.

Skovholt, Thomas. 2001. *The resilient practitioner: Burnout prevention and self-care strategies for counselors, therapist, teachers, and health professionals*. Needham Heights, MA: Allyn & Bacon.

Stone, Douglas, Bruce Patton, and Sheila Heen. 2010. *Difficult conversations: How to discuss what matters most*. New York: Penguin Group.

Svinicki, Marilla, and Wilbert McKeachie. 2011. *Teaching tips*. Belmont, CA: Wadsworth.

Thiagarajan, Sivasailam. 1990. *Barnga: A simulation game on cultural clashes*. Yarmouth, ME: Intercultural Press.

Thompson, Thomas, ed. 1978. *The schooling of Native America*. Washington, DC: American Association of Colleges for Teacher Education.

Timpson, William M., and Paul Bendel-Simso. 1996. *Concepts and choices for teaching*. Madison, WI: Atwood Publishing.

Timpson, William M. 1999. *Metateaching and the instructional map*. Madison, WI: Atwood Publishing.

_____. 2002. *Teaching and learning peace*. Madison, WI: Atwood Publishing.

Timpson, William M., and Suzanne Burgoyne. 2002. *Teaching and performing: Ideas for energizing your classes*. 2nd ed. Madison, WI: Atwood Publishing.

Timpson, William M., Silvia Sara Canetto, Evelinn Borrayo, and Raymond Yang, ed. 2003. *Teaching diversity: Challenges and complexities, identities and integrity*. Madison, WI: Atwood Publishing.

Timpson, William M., Raymond Yang, Evelinn Borrayo, and Silvia Sara Canetto. 2005. *147 Tips for teaching diversity*. Madison, WI: Atwood Publishing.

Timpson, William M., Brian Dunbar, Gailmarie Kimmel, Brett Bruyere, Peter Newman, and Hilary Mizia. 2006. *147 tips for teaching sustainability: Connecting the environment, the economy and society*. Madison, WI: Atwood Publishing.

Timpson, William M., and Sue Doe. 2008. *Concepts and choices for teaching: Meeting the challenges in higher education*. Madison, WI: Atwood Publishing.

Timpson, William M., Edward J. Brantmeier, Nathalie Kees, Tom Cavanagh, Claire McGlynn, and Elavie Ndura-Ouédraogo. 2009. *147 tips for teaching peace and reconciliation*. Madison, WI: Atwood Publishing.

Tobias, Sheila. 1990. *They're not dumb, they're different: Stalking the second tier*. Tucson, AZ: Research Corporation.

Trungpa, Chögyam. 1984. *Shambhala: The sacred path of the warrior*. Boston: Shambhala.

Tuckman, Bruce W. 1965. Developmental sequence in small groups. *Psychological Bulletin*. 63(6): 384-399.

US Peace Corps. nd. About us. http://www.peacecorps.gov/about/.

Urdan, Tim, Allison M. Ryan, Eric M. Anderman, and Magaret H. Gheen. 2002. Goals, goal structures, and avoidance behaviors. In *Goals, goal structures, and patterns of adaptive learning*. Carol Midgley, ed. Mahwah, NJ: Lawrence Erlbaum Associates, 55-84.

Wade, Carole, and Carol Tavris. 2008. *Psychology*. Upper Saddle River, NJ: Pearson.

Waite, Alina M. 2009. Competitive advantage. In *The Praeger Handbook of Human Resource Management: Vol 2*. Ann Gilley, Jerry W. Gilley, Scott A. Quatro, and Pamela Dixon, ed. Westport, CT: Praeger. 333-335.

Wheatley, Margaret. 2001. *Leadership and the New Science: Discovering order in a chaotic world*. rev. ed. San Francisco: Berrett-Koehler.

Whichard, Judy, and Nathalie Kees. 2006. *The manager as facilitator*. Westport, CT: Praeger.

Williams, Terry Tempest. 2009. *Finding beauty in a broken world*. New York: Vintage.

Yang, Raymond. 2003. Socratic and therapeutic Underpinnings of Self-Disclosure in the Classroom. In *Teaching diversity: Challenges and complexities, identities and integrity*. William M. Timpson, Silvia Sara Canetto, Evelinn A. Borrayo, and Raymond Yang, ed. Madison, WI: Atwood Publishing. 77-90.

Young, Nicholas D., and Christine N. Michael, ed. 2010. *Creative Solutions to contemporary challenges in small and rural school across America*. Weston, MA: Learning Disabilities Worldwide.